HEAVEN AND HELL WITHIN

PART II

Karmic Personality Development

notionpress.com

INDIA • SINGAPORE • MALAYSIA

HEAVEN AND HELL WITHIN

PART II

Karmic Personality Development

HIMANSHU SHANGARI

notionpress.com

INDIA • SINGAPORE • MALAYSIA

Notion Press

No.8, 3rd Cross Street,
CIT Colony, Mylapore,
Chennai, Tamil Nadu – 600004

First Published by Notion Press 2020

ISBN 978-93-5206-441-0

ॐ

Om Namah Shivaay

This book has become possible with the Grace of Lord Shiva and each valuable word in it is due to his blessings.

Om Namah Shivaay

CONTENTS

They Come First

After bowing to Lord Shiva, let me take this moment to bow to the person who has been a very strong and supportive influence in my life. She is my respected and adorable mother, **Smt. Jeewan Lata**. So much can be said about her contribution to my life, that a whole book can be written about it. However, I will simply say that even an ocean of words can't describe her true contribution to my life.

After that, I bow to my dear and respected father **Lt. Sh. Bodh Raj Shangari**. Though he left us when I was nine only, the mere fact that he along with my mother brought me to this world, makes me indebted to him for this life as well as for the lives to come. God bless your soul father, wherever you are! Though you are physically not with me, you are always there with me and in me, through all the sweet memories of my childhood, and you will always be.

PRELUDE

So many books have been written on the topic of personality development that some people may think there is no need for more books. In reality, we need more and more books on this topic. This is because if each book is able to give you even one valuable tip to improve yourself, which you didn't know before, the purpose of writing and reading the book has been served.

Human race is ever evolving. With continuous evolution, new researchers come up with new ideas and theories in various spheres of life, from time to time. Though many of them don't seem to deny theories established before their time, they add new values to the already existing theories so that we may benefit more from such theories.

However, some researchers do come up with new theories related to various spheres, from time to time. They offer information that was earlier not available to many. This is because a theory that holds good today may not hold equally good 100 years later, as with change in time and circumstances, the meanings and applications of various theories may change. Hence research and new information is the backbone of the process of evolution.

Personality development is a vast and complex sphere, as there is much more to it than appears on the surface. In order to improve yourself, you should first learn what lies inside of you, since it's easy to change something when you know what it is.

This book deals with habits which can affect your performance in negative ways, as well as create many problems in various spheres of your life. These habits include Being too Possessive, Lack of Concentration, Lack of Determination, Too many Grudges, Lack of Trust and some other negative habits.

A number of readers sent requests to include the topic of rebirth and liberation in this part. Hence a chapter on rebirth has also been included. This chapter includes the reasons why we're born again and again. It also explains what the state of liberation is and how it can be reached.

Lord Shiva Bless You

Himanshu Shangari

Being too Possessive

Teing too possessive is a habit due to which you don't want to let go of people, things and/or places which you want for yourself or which you consider are yours.

Though this problem can cause problems in every sphere of life, it may cause maximum damage in the sphere of relationships. If you suffer from this problem, you may tend to control the lives of the people who are in relationships with you like your friends, girlfriend, wife, children, siblings and other relatives.

Taking an example, if you have this habit, you may keep telling your girlfriend what to do and what not to, where to go and where not to, who to meet and who not to and many other dos and don'ts. You subconsciously assume that you have the right to do so whereas in reality, no one holds the right to control anyone's life and actions. As you keep putting pressure on her, she may feel more and more uncomfortable with time; and she may break up with you when she can't handle this habit of yours any longer.

Let's first try to understand what possession is. Possession is the original sin and it is in the root of all evil. You can't engage in a bad karma without being possessive. At times, such possession may be obvious which means conscious. At other times, it may be so subtle or subconscious that you may not realize it is there, despite your best efforts.

To possess someone or something means you want him/it to be something else. Considering a person, it means that you don't accept him for what he is and you want him to change, even if he doesn't want to. When you have such desire, you're going against the primary rule of nature, which is the right of freewill for each and every soul.

You try to change people so that they may become such versions of themselves which you like and/or which will be more convenient for you. In doing so, you're ignoring the fact they have freewill. Hence whether or not they want to change, is their choice and not yours. When you engage in one such practice, you're treating a person like a thing. For example, your cellphone doesn't have a wish of its own and you can change a number of settings, as and when you want. The cellphone doesn't have freewill and hence it has no objections to whatever you make of it.

Likewise, you may customize your car, computer, room, sofa, bed and a number of other things, the way you want to. However, when it comes to people, they're not things and they have freewill. When you try to change them without their own will, you treat them like things or objects, instead of treating them as people.

In the deepest sense, you can't change anyone or anything without possessing such person or thing. Such possession may not always be physical or visible and it may be subtle at times. Taking an example, suppose you forbid your wife to meet certain specific people or visit certain specific places. It is visible possession as even you may see that you're trying to change her against her will, which means you're trying to restrict her choices. Since it should be her choice and not yours, you're possessing her.

Looking at another example, you don't forbid your wife from meeting specific people but you keep telling her that you don't like them and you really wish she didn't meet them. Though she is free to make this choice whether or not to meet them; you're influencing her choice by constantly telling her that you want her not to do so. Hence you're possessive though this possession is relatively subtle.

Going deeper, you don't forbid her and you don't even repeatedly advise her that you don't like certain people she meets. However, you keep wishing that she shouldn't meet them. Whenever she has bad experiences with one of them and she shares them with you, you feel happy and you encourage her to share more and more of such experiences. In this case, you may or may not advise her to stay away from such person, depending on your stage of evolution. Though all you may do is wish, listen and enjoy; you're possessive.

As discussed in the chapter 'Transfer of energy through Karmas' of the book 'Heaven and Hell Within Part 01'; a karma is decided by the intention behind it and not by its outward expression. In this case, there may be no outward expression from your side. It means you may never tell her to move away from such people that you don't like. However, a desire/intention for the same is always there in your mind. It means that though your problem of being possessive is very subtle in this case, it is still there.

This theory applies to everyone and everything. You can't engage in any bad karma at all, without being possessive on one level or another. Looking at it from another angle, whenever you wish to possess something or someone, you're creating problems. Let's take some other examples to understand this concept in a better manner. Suppose you wish to cheat someone for money. In order to do so, you have to have this desire that he co-operates in being cheated. Though such desire may be subconscious in most cases, it is there.

This is because you want money by cheating this person and this task can't be accomplished if he's smart enough to see through your trick. Hence you consciously or subconsciously wish that he should be fool enough to fall for your trick. When you do so, you wish to make the other person what he may not be or what he may not wish to be. It means you're trying to possess him or change him.

Taking another example, suppose it's raining for three days and you're tired of it. Hence you wish that it stops since you don't like it now or you may be facing problems because of it. The moment you make such wish, you're trying to change the elements of nature, which means you're trying to possess nature. Without such possession, you can't change them. This is an even subtler form of possession but it is possession.

Similarly, you may wish winter to be not too cold this year as you don't like winters. In wishing so, you're possessive because you wish to change the course of nature according to your own convenience. Likewise, if you don't wish to look older, you don't wish to die or you have other similar wishes related to your body, you're possessive. Such acts of possession are very subtle but they are there. You're not accepting yourself for what you are or for what you're becoming; and you wish to impose your choices on natural changes. It means you wish to control nature. Since you can't change anything without possessing it first, you're trying to possess nature as well as your body.

It means that deep down; possession means the opposite of acceptance. You can be possessive, only if you're not able to accept people and/or things for what they are and you want to change them, so that they're more suitable for you. On the other hand, if you are able to accept everyone and everything, you don't wish to change anyone or anything. Hence you're free from possession. When you're completely free from possession, you're liberated.

Each and every desire/resolution remains there in your subconscious because you've consciously possessed it. Hence you have to be possessive in order to create desires and hold on to them. It means possession lies in the root of all desires and resolutions. Looking at good karmas; you engage in them and you create desires for good results. By doing so, you're being possessive since you can't create and maintain desires without being possessive.

Looking at bad karmas; you can't engage in any one of them in the deepest sense; without being possessive. Even when you want to hurt someone, it is because you don't like the way he behaves and you wish to change it. Hence you're possessive. For example, you may hit your wife because she doesn't quit drinking despite your repeated advice or you may hit her because she keeps telling you to quit drinking. You're possessive in both the cases.

In the first case, you want her to quit drinking and you have no regard for her free will. Looking at it from another angle, it means that you can't accept her for what she is and you want to change her into someone that you like. Hence you're possessive. In the second case, you're again not giving her the choice to tell you that she doesn't like it when you drink. Hence you want her to stop giving you advice. It means you are not able to accept her the way she is and you want to change her into someone who's more suitable for you. Hence you're treating her as an object as you're trying to customize her according to your choices. It means you're possessive.

Taking another example, suppose you try to rob someone, he opposes and you injure him. The reason you want to rob him is that you can't accept your current financial situation and you want to make it better by robbing other people. It means you're engaging in this bad karma because you want to control your situation. You injure this person as he tries to fight you. It means you injured him because he went against your wish which was that he should have co-operated. Here again, you're trying to customize this person and you're not giving him freewill.

If you can accept your financial situation, you don't need to engage in such bad karmas. Likewise, if you accept your wife's habit of drinking or her habit of saying things to you when you're drunk; you don't need to hit her. It means once acceptance comes, possession has to go. Since you're able to accept everything and everyone as they are and you don't wish to make any changes; you're liberated.

This is why liberated people don't judge anyone. In order to judge, you have to first consider that there may be something wrong with them. Through judgment, you want them to change if needed; which means you have to possess them. That's why it is said that God loves you and accepts you with all your goodness and flaws. Since he's not possessive, he doesn't have the choice to make changes to you. In other words, he can't accept parts of you and reject parts of you. Hence he's able to accept a saint as well as a sinner in the same manner. He's comfortable with the fact that the saint is doing what he likes and the sinner is doing what he likes. Both of them are practicing their right of using freewill and God's fine with it.

This topic is vast and even an entire book is not sufficient to cover it. Hence let's get back to the points that we need to deal with. Though the element of possession is there within most of us; the percentage of this element decides how troublesome it can be. If it is there but it is low in percentage; it may not be an issue for you.

As discussed in the first part of this book; for most habits/traits, there are habits/traits which lie in opposition to them. The sum total of two opposite habits/traits is always 100. It was discussed that if you're 80% kind, you're 20% selfish. Likewise, if you're 70% ruled by ego, you're 30% ruled by conscience. In the same way, if the element of possession is 20%, that of acceptance is 80% within you. In such case, you're an evolved soul and this much possession may not cause problems for you. With this percentage of possession, you may only wish that some people or some things were different than they are; and you may not engage in speech or actions to change them. Hence you may not face problems since such possession may not be strong enough to make you engage in bad karmas of significant quantum.

Moving on, the share of possession and acceptance may be 50–50 within you. It means you're significantly possessive but not highly possessive. Hence you may engage in acts of possession at times and you may accept people or things how they are, at times. As the element of possession increases in percentage, you may face more and more problems. Hence you should start dealing with it if you know or find out that being possessive is causing problems.

Let's look at some symptoms that various people suffering from this problem may have. Many such people may not retire their old clothes, shoes and other likewise items. They may keep purchasing new ones and they may not get rid of the old ones. It should be noted that keeping used clothes and other likewise items for 3, 4 or 5 years may not be a problem; especially when you're using them.

There may be some items that you wish to keep even after 10 years or more. This is fine as long as it is not a pattern. It means if you're keeping most of your clothes for many years even when you don't use them and you don't have intentions to use them; you're possessive. The clothes belong to you and you don't want them to belong to anyone else. Hence you may keep them as long as you're able to. The same may apply to shoes, watches, books, medicines, supplements and a number of other items. Here again, as long as you're using them or you intend to use them, it should be fine. When you don't use them and you also know that you're not going to use them but you still keep them; it's a problem.

Let's look at some other likewise items which may be different for various people. Such people may keep perfume bottles many of which may be empty or they may contain small amounts of contents. They may have old coins and/or currency notes which are no longer used, old wallets, handbags, purses, old and useless lipsticks, nail colour bottles many of which may be empty, shaving razors, old hair bands, ribbons, audio cassettes, CDs and a number of other such items. Here again, they may not use these things and they may not have any intentions of using them.

However, they may still retain these items, as they may not wish to part with them.

Likewise, they may have old electrical wires, old telephone cables, old telephone sets, mobile handsets, partly broken or damaged furniture items, useless batteries and a number of other such things which have lost relevance but they are still retaining them. Here again, you may keep one or two of these items for many years and you may still not have this problem. This is because such items may carry emotional value for you. Hence such items may be physically useless but they're emotionally useful. For instance, you may have your first watch with you which your father bought you 50 years ago. Though the watch may be useless now, it reminds you of your father's love for you. Hence it is not useless and it is useful.

However, if this practice forms a pattern and you retain most of the things that you purchase or obtain; long after they've lost their relevance, you have problem of being possessive. It means with conscious efforts, you've written a script on your subconscious that you don't wish to let go of anything that belongs to you. As a result, you become naturally/subconsciously good at holding on to things, even long after they've lost relevance.

As this habit aggravates, it may expand to other spheres of your life. For example, you may refuse to lend your car to a friend for a couple of days when he has valid reason to borrow it and you have an extra car. Though he may be a close friend and you may even try hard to give him your car, you may not be able to do so. This is because your subconscious may send strong signals of discomfort when it comes to part with your car, even for two days. Hence you may end up refusing him and you may even regret later. If you've reached this stage, it means the problem has become too strong to handle for your conscious mind.

On conscious level, you may wish to give him your car as you value this friendship. However, your conscious desire may not be able to compete with the script written on your subconscious and you may end up refusing him. Likewise, you may often refuse to lend money to your friends or relatives, even when you have a lot to spare and they need it a lot. Even if you put in a lot of conscious effort and you lend money to one such friend despite your gut feeling (subconscious) saying 'no'; you may start feeling uncomfortable soon after that.

Hence you may start reminding your friend that he owes you money, even when the promised deadline is far away. You may even ask him to return your money before the time promised by him; and you may present excuses. It means you may create fake need for such money and tell him to return it. Likewise, you may take similar actions related to other things that you possess.

With time, your friends and relatives may learn this fact that material things mean much more to you than they do. Hence they may re-evaluate their relationships with you. As a result, most of them may start maintaining distance from you and they may also present excuses when you're in need. Some of them may have different natures and they may choose to have no relationship with you. Hence you may lose such friends.

This habit can drive your loved ones away in other ways also. For example, if you have a girlfriend, you may try to possess her also like many other things you possess and in doing so, you may push her away from yourself. Whenever she talks to some other guy, you may feel uncomfortable as you consider her as one of your possessions and you don't have a habit of sharing your possessions with other people or letting go of your possessions. This habit gives birth to a fear which says that the other guy may take her away from you and you may have to part with such a dear possession.

As this fear gets stronger, you may tell her that she should not talk to this guy and in order to convince her, you may give her many reasons why should she not talk to him. Your girlfriend may feel uncomfortable with your approach. Since it may be your first time or one of the first few times you have done such a thing to her, she may accept your wish and stop talking to that guy. As the time goes by, you may keep telling her not to speak to this guy, that guy and many other guys. As the number of guys she can't speak to increases, her level of discomfort may also increase. Hence she may feel the need to move away from you as you are restricting her choices or freewill according to your wish and this is something no one likes.

Hence she may decide to keep talking to many such guys, you may have asked her not to talk to. This may create tension between the two of you and you may try even harder to convince her not to talk to these guy. She may also do many other things which you may have told her to stop doing. Harder you try to stop her, worse your situation may become and a point may come when your girlfriend may find you too much to handle. Hence she may decide to move away from you or break up with you.

Similarly, you may keep investigating her social media activities and you may keep asking her about her equations with some people she's been interacting with, through one of her social networking profiles. You may demand more and more explanations about who these people are, why she's speaking or chatting with them, and all other such questions which convey the message to her that you doubt and restrict her. Hence she may start feeling more and more uncomfortable and restricted in this relationship.

Finally a stage may come when driven by your continuous doubts and restrictions, she may break up with you. Instead of realizing your mistake, you may think that your doubts were true and she was not loyal to you. Such thoughts may provide even more strength to your habit of being too possessive. The reason she left is that you tried to hold on to her too tight. However, the reason you may assume is that you were not able to hold on to her properly and that is why she slipped. This belief may create the need to be more thorough when investigating the affairs of your next girlfriend.

As a result, you may investigate the affairs of your next girlfriend with even more intensity which may cause even more problems. Hence you may end up losing this girlfriend also. This trend may continue and no girlfriend may settle with you. This is because you're trying to treat them as objects or things which don't have freewill and they can be customized in any way you want. However, they are people and they have freewill. Hence you can't possess them like you possess things.

Likewise, you can't control them like you control things. For example, you may tell your car to be there in the garage and it'll not leave until you want it to. The same doesn't hold well in case of people, since they may do what they wish and not what you want them to do. Sooner you learn this fact and stop controlling them, better it is.

Looking at some activities to treat this habit, start releasing your possessions one by one and start from a small scale. At the first level, start giving away your old and useless clothing items or any other such items mentioned before that you have retained even when you don't have any use for them. In order to get best results, either give these items to needy people if they can still be used by someone, or throw them away if they can't be used by anyone at all, instead of exchanging them for something in return. Don't give away many of your old items in a single go during the first level and give them away one by one after regular intervals of time.

Giving away many items at once may create strong discomfort within you. Remember, more an act is in opposition to the script written on your subconscious, stronger resistance the subconscious may pose. Hence you may feel uncomfortable and you may regret your decision. You may even choose to disengage from this practice and in the worst case, you may try to get some of your possessions back. Hence start with small offerings. Small acts don't stand in strong opposition to the script of possession written on your subconscious mind. Hence the subconscious may pose mild resistance and you may be able to overcome such resistance with conscious effort.

As you give away more and more items, your conscious mind sends more and more messages to your subconscious that you wish to release. Since releasing is the opposite of possessing, such messages may start reducing the quantum of this habit. With time and efforts, you may reach a stage when your subconscious mind may not send vibes of discomfort whenever you engage in acts of giving away your possessions. It means you've mastered this level and you're ready for the next level.

During the next level, start sharing some of your useful possessions with your friends and relatives. Don't share things which you love a lot and start with the ones that you can afford to share at this time, though with some difficulty. For example, if you love your car as well as your money a lot; don't share them with your friends at this stage. Doing so may trigger resistance from your subconscious, which may be too strong for you to handle at this stage. Hence stay away from such practices.

On the other hand, if you feel that you may share your clothes, shoes, some of your gadgets and other items with some difficulty; you should start sharing them. At every level, the idea is to do something which is somewhat but not a lot more difficult than what you're accustomed to. It is like if you're comfortable lifting 100 kg at gym; you may choose to go for 110 or 120 and not for 150 or 200 as you may fail. With time and efforts, you may reach 150 also, but it is not wise to attempt it at this stage. Hence 110 is a wiser choice. Apply the same theory here and move up slowly.

With time and efforts, you may feel comfortable with this level also. It means you should move to the next level. At this level, increase the resistance and start sharing more. By this time, significant changes have been made to the script written on your subconscious mind. Hence it may not pose strong resistance for this level now. Looking at an activity for this level, if a friend asks for your car for a couple of days and you can afford to do so with some conscious effort, you should lend it to him. You may still have some discomfort but it may not be a lot and you may get over it with some conscious effort.

Similarly, start sharing such things at this level, which are not the dearest ones but which are dear to you. With efforts and time, you may get through this level also and you may be ready for the next level. During the next level, start sharing your dearest possessions with friends and relatives. For example, if you love money the most; start lending it to friends and relatives when they need it. Be careful not to lend money to anyone and everyone, merely in order to complete this activity. Assess the need of the person in question as well as his personality and take a calculated decision.

For example, if a friend asks for money and you know that he has a reputation of not returning money, be careful. Either don't lend him any money or lend as much as you can afford to part with. For instance, if you can afford to give him USD 100 and forget this amount without hurting your friendship, in case he doesn't return it; you should give him this amount and not more than that. If you can't afford to lose USD 500 and you know the friend may not return it; don't give him this amount as you may lose money as well as friend.

Hence be wise when you're sharing money or valuables with other people. As you engage in more and more such acts; your conscious mind may replace the remaining parts of the script on your subconscious, with time and efforts. Finally, a stage may come when you may get rid of unhealthy amounts of possession. Though you may still be somewhat possessive but such possession may not manifest on physical levels in most cases. Your habit of being too possessive has been cured and you may continue to grow more and more from here.

Looking at parallel measures, start applying these practices to your personal life also, from third level onward. It means when you're ready to lend your car to a friend in need, you should start giving space to your girlfriend, wife, children, friends and other likewise people. Let them make their choices and try not to interfere much. For example, don't bother much when your girlfriend talks to some other guys or she opts to have male friends. She has a right to her own life and she can live it the way she wants, until she crosses a line. Be wise enough to know when a line is crossed and don't be alarmed by small things.

On the contrary, you can promote and support her in doing such acts. For example, you can encourage her to make more male friends if you feel that she wants to do so and she is abstaining only because she is afraid that she may offend you or make you uncomfortable. Simply take a step forward and encourage her to do so and let her know that you trust her, and her happiness as well as freedom is important for you. You should try and do the same to your wife, husband, boyfriend, children, friends and/or relatives; and you should give them more freedom and space whenever it is needed.

You may think that by giving this much freedom and space to your girlfriend or boyfriend, you are risking your relationship as he or she may find a person better than you and he or she may leave you for them. In reality, this is just a fear and nothing else and you are not going to lose your girlfriend to some other guy by doing so, if she really likes you. On the contrary, she may respect and love you more.

Contrary to what some people may think, your girlfriend or boyfriend, your husband or wife, are not always looking for better people or better choices. For example, your girlfriend may not leave you for a better person in most cases, if you are a good enough person or even a reasonable person to be with. Your girlfriend may leave you for someone else only if you are not a good person, you don't respect her enough, love her enough, care for her enough or you lack many other such good qualities. If such is the case, she is anyway going to leave you sooner or later, no matter whether you allow her some freedom or not. By restricting her, you're only going to make her leave you sooner.

Most people may not always be on the lookout for the best partner in the world. They may not wish to run from one person to another in search of better and better people, until they have reached the best person. Most people may wish to settle in their lives when they find someone good enough for them, though this someone may not be the best person or a very good person. It is only in a case when a person is not good enough for someone or not good at all, that the second person starts looking for other options as she may not want to waste her life with someone who is not capable of adding any value to it.

People love freedom and they are generally not comfortable with anyone who tries to restrict it. Freewill is the basic expression of every soul and no one should try to restrict it. The best way to avoid someone leaving you is by not holding them. In order for someone to leave you, you must hold them first. Holding here means that you get possessive beyond healthy limits. As you do so, this creates a need for them to take a step back. On the contrary, most people love such people who are liberating type and they provide freedom to everyone in their circle. Just imagine why would you want to leave someone who gives you complete freedom and accepts you for what you are?

Therefore, if many of your girlfriends have left you for other people and you are afraid of giving any freedom to your current girlfriend, fearing that she may also find someone else and run away, you are not treating your problem and you are making it worse. This is because, you are trying to hold on to her so tightly and block her breathing space so much that she has no choice left but to push you away or move away from you so that she may get some comfort. Hence, restricting her freedom and being too possessive is only making your problem worse.

If many of your girlfriends have left you, the fault probably doesn't lie in them and it lies in you. Hence instead of finding more ways to stop your current girlfriend from running away, you should find more ways to fix yourself and make yourself a better person who can add some value to his girlfriend's life. If you are good enough to provide value to your girlfriend and make her happy, she may not leave you. However, if you have many negative habits and you can only make your girlfriend feel uncomfortable and miserable in your company, you may not be able to stop her from leaving you no matter what tricks you may try.

As you allow more freedom to the people around you, and as you motivate as well as support them to make the most of their lives, they may start respecting and loving you more. This is the time when you realize that more you try to possess a person, more he moves away from you whereas more you liberate a person from conditions, closer he gets. So what is possession according to you, may actually work as a runaway signal for most people around you whereas what is freedom or letting go according to you, may actually make you possess your near and dear ones with greater strength.

Most people may do anything to ensure that they don't lose such people who are good and who encourage as well as support them to make the most of their lives. Accordingly, they tend to stay closer to such people to let them know that they hold much value in their lives and they don't want to move away from them.

Lack of Concentration

Concentration is an important factor when it comes to achieve success in various spheres of life. People who are able to concentrate on their professions, relationships and other spheres may achieve much better results than the ones who are not able to do so.

Most people who have achieved a lot in various spheres of life have done so by focusing on their targets with undivided concentration. Taking an example, a successful football player starts focusing on his game from young age, he engages in regular practice and he ensures that he pays due attention to his game. Even after achieving success, he may be focused on regular practice and all other activities which help him become better as a player.

You may have seen some players who achieve success but they are not able to hold on to it for long. Among other things, their concentration levels drop. It means they lose focus on their respective games and they are distracted by various things which come along with success. As they lose focus on the games, their performances drop and they start failing. The same may apply to almost all other people who are successful in various spheres. As long as they are focused on their objectives, they may achieve and maintain success. Once they lose focus, they may start failing. It means if you wish to achieve big things and maintain them; you need concentration/focus.

Let's now look into the problem of lack of concentration and find out what causes it. The ability to give due attention to something or someone is concentration. On the other hand, inability to give proper attention to something or someone is lack of concentration. Most people have both of them though in different ratios; like most other habits/traits lying opposite to each other. It means if your concentration level is about 90%, the factor of distraction or losing focus is 10%. Since the level of concentration is much higher than that of losing focus, you may achieve very good or great things in various spheres of life.

If this ratio is 50–50, you are stuck in the middle. It means you're able to focus at times and you're not able to focus at other times. In such cases, you may be able to focus on what you like a lot and you may not witness much focus on things or people you don't like much. As a result, you may do well in life but not more than that in most cases. If this ratio is 20–80, it means you're not able to focus on most things and people, even on the ones you like. Hence you have a serious problem of lacking concentration. As a result, you may not achieve much in most spheres of life.

Division of attention to more than one thing is the root cause of this problem. It means while engaging in one thing, you keep thinking about other things, people or situations. As you do so, your focus gets divided. Your conscious attention to anything or anyone is your concentration. More attentive you are, more is your level of concentration. When your conscious focus gets divided, you're not able to give all of it to the primary task in question.

Taking an example, suppose you're trying to prepare for an exam. As you start studying, your mind may start wandering in many directions. Since you have only one mind and it has limited abilities though such limits may be big or very big, the amount of focus that you can put on study is reduced. For instance, 50% of your attention is there for study and the remaining 50% may be focused on your girlfriend, football or other likewise things/people. As a result, you may not be able to prepare well and you may not achieve good results.

It means that if you can find a way to be focused on thing at a time and you can learn how not to let your attention get divided, you may get out of this problem. The reason you're not able to give your undivided attention to most objectives is that your subconscious mind has a script of attending to more than one objective at a time. In simple words, you have a habit of attending to more than one thing at a time. Due to such script, your subconscious poses resistance whenever you wish to focus on an objective.

Let's see how this script is written. You write it with repeated conscious acts of engaging in more than one job at a time. For example, you may watch television or do something else while you're eating or drinking something. Let's say you watch television when you have your major meals. Eating meals is the primary objective here, since you can do well by not watching television but not by not having meals. Hence your undivided attention should go to having and enjoying a meal while you're having it.

However, you may pay 80% attention to the television and only 20% attention to the meal. This sends a message to your subconscious that you don't wish to focus completely on the primary objective and you're willing to distract yourself. As this message is sent again and again, the subconscious registers it. Hence you may start having craving for television whenever you're having a meal.

A meal may not be important for you on conscious level, the subconscious assigns utmost importance to it. This is because it knows through thousands of years of experiences through various lives that eating food is one of the most important factors for survival. Hence when you choose to distract yourself consciously while eating meal, you may cause a lot of damage to your concentration. This is because when you don't wish to focus on a task which is one of the most important tasks, what else may you wish to focus on.

Food keeps you alive and it nurtures your body. It means if you're not able to pay due attention as well as respect to the act of eating; you may cause serious problems within your system. With time and repetition, your conscious mind may stop putting much effort in the act of eating food and it may put most of the effort in watching television. Hence the act of eating food may be carried out by your subconscious mind. As a reminder, your primary act is that of eating food and not that of watching television at one such time.

This is what causes damage. Drawing a comparison; suppose you're not hungry and you decide to watch a football match. When you start watching it, your primary objective is to watch this match. For fun, you may have a packet of chips or a drink while watching television. In this case also, you may put all your conscious focus on watching television and you may eat or drink with the help of your subconscious. However, the distraction caused here may not be serious or even significant. This is because your primary objective here is watching television and eating/drinking is the secondary objective. Since you're paying utmost conscious attention to the act of watching television, you may not create problems here, since you're focused on your primary objective.

When you're having a major meal, the equation reverses. Your primary objective is to have such meal and television is secondary which means distraction. Since you're paying most of your conscious attention to distraction than paying it to your primary objective, you may create problems through this act. Though you seem to do the same thing in both cases; you're not. In one case, you're focusing on your primary objective whereas in the other case, you're trying your best not to focus on your primary objective. This is what causes the problem. Hence watching television doesn't cause this problem; watching it when you shouldn't be, causes it.

Likewise, you may talk on cellphone while driving your car. The primary objective here is to drive the car and cellphone is secondary which means distraction. However, you let your subconscious drive the car and you put a lot of conscious effort in the act of talking to someone over phone. This is another practice which you may engage in on regular basis. Through it, your conscious mind sends repeated messages to your subconscious to the effect that you like being distracted when doing something.

Let's look at some other activities which you may engage in regularly and which may create as well as aggravate this problem. Morning tea or coffee is an important activity if you do so. This is the first energy providing meal of your day and hence it should be given utmost importance. However, you read newspaper or you may reply to messages on your phone, while having tea or coffee. Here again, having tea/coffee is the primary activity and newspaper or messages are distractions. Hence this activity contributes towards lack of concentration.

Taking another example, you read newspaper and at the same time, you start talking to someone over phone. Reading newspaper is primary activity and talking over phone is distraction in this case, since you consciously chose to read newspaper. While you were reading it, you thought of calling someone or someone called you and you started doing both the jobs. Hence you're contributing to the problem through this activity.

Looking at another practice, whenever you call someone to discuss something, you engage in something else. For example, you may start reading newspaper, watching television or engaging in some domestic task. Here again, calling someone is the primary task since you consciously chose to call him/her; whereas all other tasks are distractions. Hence you're aggravating your problem.

Likewise, you talk to people while lifting weights at gym. It may be fine if you do so when you have small breaks in between. However, if you're talking to people while you doing weight training, you're aggravating this problem. Here again, your primary task is to engage in weight training and talking to people is distraction. Similarly, talking over phone while cooking, eating or drinking something while driving, chatting over Whatsapp while you're in a discussion with someone or while someone is telling you something important, talking to fellow students when teacher is delivering lecture and a number of other such activities may create/aggravate the problem of lack of concentration.

You may realize that you engage in a number of such activities on daily basis. Such activities write a script of distraction or lack of concentration on your subconscious mind, through repetition and over time. Once such script is written, the subconscious starts executing it. When that happens, you may start doing all such things naturally. Hence you may not even realize that you have to watch television while eating, you have to talk to someone over phone while driving or cooking; and you have to do many other such things which are distractions. In other words, even you may not realize that you have developed a habit of engaging in more than one job at a time. The habit of engaging in more than one job at a time causes lack of concentration.

Hence you develop this habit and you may be fine with it most of the time since you may love such distractions. However every now and then, you are supposed to engage in tasks which are important and which need your undivided attention. Hence you try your best to do so but you fail. This happens because you have a habit of doing more than one thing at a time and you're trying to go against this habit. As a result, your subconscious poses resistance since you're going against the script written on it.

Hence you may not be able to concentrate, as your subconscious may create various types of distractions. As you lose concentration due to such distractions, the results may be compromised and you may not achieve success. If you've ever wondered why you were not able to give your undivided attention to some important tasks even when you tried your best to do so; now you know the reason. Hence you don't need to try harder to focus; you need to change the script on your subconscious.

In old times; a specific place for eating major meals was chosen in every house. All members went to that specific place at the time of eating their meals. No one watched anything and no one was supposed to talk to anyone while eating. Many families thanked God for blessing them with food. This entire practice was in place to make sure that when you engage in one of the most important activities of your life; you give it your undivided attention. Hence every member was consciously aware that he's engaging in an important task and he needs to focus on it completely.

This small but important activity sent messages that when engaging in important activities; distractions are not welcome. Likewise, people used to implement this method in most other spheres of their lives and they didn't engage in more than one job at a time. As a result, they had better focus and they were more peaceful.

Distraction will almost always disturb peace since peace is the quality of being completely present at one place as well as being in complete harmony with one place or situation. When distraction arrives, this condition is violated, since you're present at more than one place or situation at a time. Hence you not only lose focus, you start losing peace of mind also.

This is one of the reasons that with the introduction of more and more means of distraction like televisions, internet and cellphones; people are becoming more and more restless with time. When you have many things to attend to; you may be anything but peaceful. Since you're divided between many things, people and situations; you violate the primary condition of being peaceful.

Now that we've understood the root cause of this problem; let's look at ways to fix it. There are broadly two reasons due to which you may lack focus. The first one is that you may be trying to do something which you don't like at all or you dislike it. When you do so, your subconscious opposes you even if your concentration level is otherwise good. This is because almost everyone has written strong script of 'stay away from things/people you don't like' on his/her subconscious.

Hence when you engage in such tasks, your subconscious may send you strong feelings of repulsion and it may try to distract you in various ways. As a result, you may not perform well. An effective way to get rid of lack of concentration in this case is to stay away from things/people you don't like at all or dislike. Try to engage in tasks which you like and this problem should go away. If at times, you have to engage in such tasks or with such people who you don't like; you may be able to focus more if your concentration in general is very good. In addition to that, good level of determination may help a lot in such cases.

Looking at the second and major reason, you have a script of 'engage in more than one thing at a time', on your subconscious mind. Hence you need to rewrite this script to 'one thing at a time' in order to get rid of this problem. As you engage in more and more conscious acts of doing one thing at a time; the script may change and you may achieve higher levels of concentration.

To start with, make sure that you don't do anything else when you eat. Don't watch television and don't talk to anyone. At the first level, try to focus on food as much as you can, while eating it. For instance, put conscious focus on the acts of taking food from your plate, putting it in your mouth, feeling its texture and enjoying its taste. Try to engage yourself as much as you can and try to feel your food as much as you can. With time and efforts, you may start enjoying your food much more than before.

Along with this, make sure that you stop all other such activities where you engage in more than one task at a time. Some of these activities have already been mentioned before. Be consciously aware that whenever you engage in a task; you don't do anything else. For instance, don't talk over phone while cooking and don't read newspaper while having tea/coffee. Likewise, don't reply to text messages while talking to someone.

While driving car, don't talk over phone. If you have to receive an important phone call, park your car on the side of road, receive the call and then resume driving. In case you don't have the option of parking your car and you have to receive an important call, carry handsfree Bluetooth device or another likewise device which may reduce the distraction a lot. At the same time, make the call as short as you can and always go for the option of parking your vehicle on the side, whenever this option is available. Talking through handsfree devices should be a reserved option and it should be used in case of emergencies only, when no other option is available.

Though you're distracted when you talk through handsfree devices; such distraction may be less or much less compared to when you hold your phone against your ear and talk. You're driving car, you're holding phone and you're talking. It means you're engaging in three activities at a time. In addition to that, holding the phone with your hand can restrict one hand and you need both hands to drive effectively. Hence handsfree devices are better if you have to take important calls while driving.

As you engage in all such activities with conscious effort to do one thing at a time; such efforts send messages to your subconscious. With time, these messages start replacing the existing script on the subconscious with the new script. As the new script starts taking effect, you may feel that your concentration levels are increasing. You can build up more and more from here.

You don't need to work to fix bigger things and all you need to do is to make sure that you take care of the small day to day activities. Once you've mastered the art of doing one thing at a time in your day to day activities; you may find that you're able to focus naturally/subconsciously when it comes to important tasks. It means the script on your subconscious has been replaced and you now have good levels of concentration instead of having lack of concentration.

Lack of Determination

Determination is an important habit/trait as it can help you a lot in most spheres of life. On the contrary, lack of determination can cause problems in most spheres of your life.

Determination in this context means that once you've decided to do or not do something, you stick to your decision no matter what comes. For this reason, most of the successful people in various spheres have a lot of it. Without determination, it may simply not be possible to achieve big or very big goals. The essence of determination lies in the fact that once you've made a conscious decision, you don't change it unless circumstances so demand.

Taking an example, suppose you have a project at work and you are supposed to complete it within 15 days. You're determined to finish it within time and you do so. However if for some reason, the project is dropped or the timeline is extended, you may choose to drop it or finish it according to the new timeline. On the other hand, if you lack determination, you may not be able to complete it within 15 days, even when your office demands so.

Taking another example, suppose you've decided to go for walk, every day at 6 in the morning. Hence you get up early and follow this routine. In case you fall sick, you sleep very late due to some reason or you have some other task on a particular day at the same time, you choose not to go for walk. It means you're determined and you change this decision only when the circumstances demand. On the other hand, if you get up and go for walk at times and you don't do so at times, without any valid reasons and because of not feeling like going, you may lack determination.

Let's look at the root cause of lack of determination. Conscious acts of not sticking to your objectives when you should, form a script of lack of determination on your subconscious mind. For example, you start reading a piece of writing which may take 20 minutes. After 5 or 10 minutes, you don't feel like reading it and you leave the rest for later. Likewise, you decide to go for walk for 20 minutes but you don't feel like doing so after 10 minutes and you quit. You decide to wash your car in the morning but when the moment comes, you don't feel like doing so and you postpone this task. You're supposed to buy groceries today but you postpone this task without valid reasons. Your car is due for service but you postpone this job as long as possible, without valid reasons.

Likewise, there are a number of other such day to day tasks which are not big or difficult to accomplish, but you still leave them without completion or you choose to postpone them. Through such conscious acts, you write a script on your subconscious that when you take a decision, you may not stick to it. Once the subconscious registers this script, it starts executing it. As a result, it may not encourage you to execute a decision or complete a task at hand. On the contrary, it may encourage you to quit or postpone. Hence you may end up quitting or postponing such task.

It may not matter much as long as it happens in small activities. Hence you may not bother much about it. Then there are some important tasks related to various spheres of life, which may appear from time to time. This is when you may try your best to complete them in proper and timely manner. However, you may fail to do so, as you may end up quitting or postponing them.

This is when you may get worried as to why you are not able to complete such tasks despite your best efforts. Your subconscious recognizes you as a person who doesn't stick to most of his decisions and who doesn't complete most tasks in proper/timely manner. Hence it discourages and distracts you on account of various reasons. When that happens, your mind gets divided. Your conscious wants to finish this task whereas your subconscious wants to quit/postpone it. Since the subconscious is much stronger than the conscious in most cases, you may end up quitting/postponing it.

Determination is a unique quality which defines the equation of dominance between your subconscious and conscious mind. More determined you are, better are the chances that you may be able to do whatever you consciously decide, despite resistance posed by your subconscious mind. For this reason, determined people may improve their negative habits much faster than people who are not determined. Taking an example, a non-determined person may need 6 months to quit smoking, doing so step by step. On the other hand, a determined person may do so in a matter of days.

Quitting here means doing so effectively. Hence quitting today and starting tomorrow doesn't count for quitting. For this reason, a non-determined person may need to reduce the number of cigarettes he smokes per day, step by step after regular intervals. Let's say such interval is 15 days. It means he's able to reduce 2 cigarettes per day, after every 15 days. A determined person may reduce 5 cigarettes per day, at intervals of 7 days or less. A person with strong determination may decide one day that he won't smoke at all from the moment in question and the chapter is closed.

The quality of determination decides how seriously your subconscious should take your conscious mind. If you have average amount of determination, you may need a number of conscious acts repeated over a period of time to change a script on your subconscious. Looking at the other extreme, you may simply send a message to your subconscious that you wish to change a habit and it's done.

Such extreme levels of determination are found in people who're spiritually very advanced. With practice, they've made their conscious minds so powerful that their subconscious minds don't need repeated acts to listen to them. Their conscious wishes are so strong that they alone can change the scripts written on their subconscious minds. When conscious mind registers a command with the subconscious, it attaches priority to such command. The subconscious pays utmost attention to such priority.

Hence the commands which are low in priority need to be repeated again and again, over a period of time, in order for the subconscious to take them seriously. However, the commands which have been forward with tags of high priority are dealt with at the earliest. Have you wondered why a person who's afraid of physical fights may be prepared to fight till death if his own life or that of a loved one is in danger?

This person is not brave in general. Hence if he wishes to develop bravery, he may need to send repeated messages through conscious acts of bravery. Such messages don't carry much intensity and hence they need to be repeated. When this person faces a do or die situation, his conscious mind asks for bravery with such intensity that the subconscious may not need to be asked twice. This is why people may behave very differently from their standard behaviour patterns when they face extreme situations. Their conscious minds are so focused and determined during such times that whatever they convey to their subconscious minds, is dealt with on high priority.

A highly determined person enjoys this state all the time. With practice, he's made his conscious mind so strong that each and every command forwarded by it to the subconscious is dealt with on high priority. This is why you may see that it is easy for some people to develop any habit or quit any habit whereas an average person may need a lot of time to do so. The former has high levels of determination whereas the latter may not have that much determination.

An interesting fact is that though determination seems to be ruled by the conscious mind, the subconscious has an important role to play. At times, there may be a clash between two or more scripts written on the subconscious. When that happens, the stronger one is given priority. Taking an example, suppose you have two scripts on your subconscious mind. The first one says you're afraid of fighting whereas the second one says you're willing to go to any limits when your life or that of a loved one is in danger.

The subconscious executes both these scripts. In general, it may discourage you when it comes to be brave. However, when you face an extreme situation, the second script may override the first script and you may show bravery for some time. Since the second script is related to survival, it may be much stronger than the first script. Hence as long as there is no clash between these scripts, which means you don't face extreme situations; the subconscious may execute the first script. The moment you face an extreme situation, it may activate the second script and it may ignore the first one.

The same may happen in case of determination, though a lot more often. When you write a script of being highly determined on your subconscious, this script may override many other scripts written on your subconscious. Since your determination levels are high, it means this script is very strong. Hence the subconscious may give it priority over most other scripts, whenever there's a clash.

Taking an example, suppose you try smoking and over a period of time, you develop a habit of smoking. You're fine with it and you don't give it a second thought. Suppose you're highly determined. It means both these scripts are running without any clash till this point. This is because you're fine with smoking and you don't wish to change this habit. Then a moment comes when you decide to quit smoking for some reason. When that happens; there's a clash between these two scripts. The script of smoking says don't quit whereas the script of determination says 'If I say quit, it means quit'.

In such situation, the subconscious will give priority to the script which is stronger. It means higher is your level of determination, stronger is its script and higher are the chances that you may be able to quit without much effort. When this script is very strong which means your level of determination is very high; you simply need to forward a command to the subconscious and it is done. Though the script of smoking may tend to pose resistance but there is no match between the strength of these two scripts.

It means as your determination levels increase, your ability to make any changes to your personality without much difficulty also increases. This is why determination is an important trait to have as it may bless you with wonderful results in the domain of materialism and at the same time, it may bless you with amazing results in the spiritual domain.

Lord Buddha is the future king, he has a beautiful and loving wife; and he has a son he loves. Then one day, he decides to leave everything in search of spiritual enlightenment and he does so effortlessly. Imagine how hard it may be to leave a kingdom as well as a loving family and lead the life of a wanderer who doesn't know whether he'll get something to eat or not. The fact that Lord Buddha executed this decision effortlessly shows how strong his determination was.

A number of scripts were clashing with each other at that moment. The love for wife, love and duty for son, responsibilities as the future king, support for the father and many other such scripts were clashing with only one script; determination. Since his determination overrode all other scripts; it must have been very strong.

Hence determination is one quality which can change the entire course of your life and to be precise; that of the journey of your soul. You can do whatever you want, you can develop any habit without much difficulty and you can quit or modify any script on your subconscious, without much effort. Stronger is your level of determination, higher are the chances that you can make any changes to your personality without much difficulty.

Let's see how determination may be developed with efforts. Begin with the basics and select a number of small day to day tasks. Then commit to yourself that you'll complete them in the manner you chose, no matter what may come. Select the easiest tasks at this level as you may not want to face strong resistance from your subconscious. For example, you may choose to read for 15 minutes every day at a specific time, wake up at a fixed time every day, walk for 15 minutes every day at a fixed time; and a number of other such activities. Choose easy activities and ensure strict compliance.

For example, if you choose to walk for 15 minutes every day and you do so effectively, your level of determination may increase. However, if you choose to walk for 30 minutes and you end up walking for 20 or 25 minutes, you may end up being less determined. Though you've walked more in the second case, you've not done what you promised to yourself. Hence when it comes to build determination, the quantity or the quantum of a task is secondary. Whether or not you're able to accomplish a task in the manner you decided, is of supreme importance.

Hence the most important factor is to select only such tasks which you can complete exactly as you decide. No matter how small they may be, they'll help. Once you're comfortable with this level, you may realize that you don't have to bother about such tasks at all and they are being done without much thought or trouble. It means you're ready for the next level.

Introduce tasks which are more but not a lot more difficult. For example, you may choose to walk for 20 minutes or read for 20 minutes instead of 15 minutes. Remember, speed is your enemy on this journey whereas patience and perseverance are your best friends. Hence don't jump levels and introduce resistance gradually. Don't jump from 15 to 30 minutes since you may not be able to do so. Hence build up slowly so that you may not face problems. Completing your tasks exactly how you decide is of primary importance and the quantum of such tasks is secondary.

As you feel comfortable with this level also, introduce new tasks which are more difficult. This way, you may introduce more difficult tasks after regular intervals. As you complete all of them in proper manner, your level of determination may increase.

At this level, you can attempt bigger tasks and the ones that matter, like those related to profession and other spheres. However, don't attempt very big tasks here as it may be early for them. Start with somewhat bigger tasks which you think you can complete with some difficulty. You can build up from here and grow more with time and efforts.

Too Many Grudges

Some people hold so many grudges within them that it becomes difficult for them to be happy. Due to such grudges, they may not perform well in many spheres of life.

This is because more grudges and frustrations you hold inside, more negative energy is added to your aura, as grudges and frustrations are negative traits and they add specific type of negative energy to your aura. This energy makes it difficult for you to perform at your best as well as be happy.

People suffering from this habit may complain about many things, people and situations around them. As this habit becomes strong, they may start having grudges about themselves also. For example, when someone asks one such person how things are at his job, he may reply that it's just all right or not good. He may add that he's not getting due credit for his work, his boss is not good, his colleagues conspire against him and/or other likewise things. He may hold the grudge that though he deserves much better, he's not getting it.

Taking another example, suppose someone asks one such person about his marriage. He may enlist a number of grudges related to marriage. He may say that despite his best efforts, it is not as good as it should be and he has to make many compromises. He may add that though he tries his best to keep his wife happy, she still finds problem to pick. He may express that he wish his marriage was better or he was married to someone better. Based on his overall personality, he may also say that may be he's not fit for her. This may happen when he has low confidence along with the habit of having grudges.

Likewise, when someone asks him about his son's performance at studies, he may express a number of grudges related to his son, his school, the education system, his wife and/or himself. He may do the same in most spheres of life. Due to such grudges, such people may become frustrated, depressed and pessimistic. Hence people around them may start avoiding them due to the negative vibes they radiate. Even you may not like to be in the company of someone who's making complaints most of the time. As more and more people move away from them, they may start having more grudges and this habit may aggravate.

Let's look at the root cause of this problem. Most such people don't have sufficient amount of confidence. As a result, they may not be able to perform a number of tasks at all or they may not be able to perform them well. Hence they may start abstaining from most such tasks. These are the ones they may want to do but they don't do because of lack of confidence and/or fear of failing and then looking like losers. As they hold themselves back more and more; grudges, regrets and complaints may build inside them and they may increase in numbers with time.

Taking an example, one such person may wish to go to a woman and ask her out for a date. However, he may lack confidence and he may not do so. Someone else may ask her out and the affected person may hold grudges against himself. Looking at another probability, he may approach the woman but she may refuse to go on a date with him due to various reasons; where his lack of confidence may be a prominent reason. In this case, he may hold grudges against the woman as well as himself.

This may happen to him again and again. He may get rejected by women and he may finally decide not to approach them even if he likes them a lot. This is when the problem may aggravate. He may hold grudges against himself for not being good enough to impress women he likes. At the same time, he may hold grudges against women in general as he may think they don't treat him well or they don't treat men well in general.

Looking at another example, you're at a party and you wish to sing. However due to fear of not performing well and being mocked, you may abstain. When you do so, you add more grudges to your subconscious, since you want to do something but you can't. Considering another scenario, you don't like something that someone does or says to you and you wish to confront him. However, you're not able to do so, likely because you lack the courage and confidence to confront this person. Hence you may hold back. This act may build more grudges. Likewise, you may build a number of grudges and regrets through many other situations.

Looking at regrets, they may almost always be built when you do something wrong or when you want to do something but you don't, due to various reasons. If you wish to do something, you try it and you give it your best; you may face failure but not regret. Once you've given something your best, regret may not be formed. Between failures and regrets, failures are much better. Failures can make you stronger if you learn from them whereas regrets may create serious problems within you. You may forget a failure the moment you achieve a success. However, you may hold a grudge or a regret, even after 25 years or more. Hence grudges and regrets are some of the worst feelings to have.

Let's look at some day to day activities which may build grudges/regrets. You wish to purchase a dress you like. However you apprehend that it may be too bold for your family or society. You get afraid that they may dislike and criticize you if you wear it. Hence you choose not to purchase such dress. This builds a regret of not buying the dress and it may build grudges against your family, society and yourself. Along with your family and society, you may also hold yourself responsible as you're not courageous enough to face them.

Hence grudges and regret have been built inside you. Whenever you come across dresses which look like the one in question or whenever you see someone wearing such dress, you may build more grudges. You may hold your family responsible for not letting you have the opportunity to wear such dresses.

These repeated acts may send messages to your subconscious that family demands sacrifices and it imposes too many expectations on you, thereby restricting your freewill. With time and through a number of other acts like this one, you may build strong grudges against your family members. As a result, you may start disagreeing and arguing more with your family members. You may disagree, dislike and/or argue more with those family members; who according to you would have criticized for most things which you didn't do, if you had done them. It means your subconscious holds them responsible for not letting you enjoy all such things.

Based on your personality, you may choose to go with one of the two options in most cases. You may either start confronting such family members more often and you may try to prove them wrong, even in situations which have got nothing to do with you. Looking at the second option, you may not have his much courage and you may start finding ways to move away from your family, so that you may live your life as you wish.

Looking at the first option, as you prove them wrong again and again, it gives you satisfaction that they are more often wrong than right. Hence they were wrong in stopping you from doing a number of things that you want to do. As that happens repeatedly, your relationship with such family members may start suffering and distance may start building between you and them. With time, this distance may increase. Finally, a stage may reach when the negative energy between you and your family members may become too much to handle. This is when the relationship is damaged seriously and in some cases, permanently.

Looking at the second option, you may not have the courage to argue with your family members and prove them wrong. However, you have grudges against them and they demand you to do something. Hence you may consciously or subconsciously start finding ways to move away from them. Many times, it happens subconsciously and even you may not know the real reason behind some of your actions.

For example, you receive a professional opportunity from a distant place or another country and you accept it at once. Though you think that you've done so because such opportunity offers good professional growth, it may not be the real reason or the only reason. Deep down, you wish to move away from your family but you don't have the courage to say it on their faces. This opportunity has come as your lucky card which you can play and get out without having to take any blames. Hence you may tell your family members how great this opportunity is and how much growth you're going to witness through it. Though your family members may think you're moving away to achieve better results in profession, you're moving away because you've built subconscious hatred for your family members through a number of grudges.

As a general rule, more grudges you hold against a person, less are the chances that you may have a healthy relationship with him. More grudges against someone means you have more reasons to dislike him. More you dislike him, more the relationship may suffer. With time, such dislike may become so strong through grudges that you may choose to break up with this person or move away from him, whichever option is available. For example, if it is a marriage or love affair, you may break up. However if it is family, you may move away since it is almost impossible to break up with family. You may move away but you may never be able to break up in the deepest sense.

More is the number of things which make you build grudges against someone, more you may dislike him and worse the relationship may become. Looking at some other activities, you wish to learn couple dance but your spouse is neither willing to learn nor willing to allow you to dance with other people from the opposite gender. Hence you may abstain from attending dance classes, though you really want to. This may build grudges inside you, against your spouse.

Likewise, you may wish to try a different and somewhat strange type of hair style. However, your family members may disapprove and they may mock or criticize you a lot if you choose to go ahead with this choice. As a result, you may either not try such hairstyle or you may switch back to your regular hairstyle, after trying the new one for some time and after receiving a lot of criticism as well as mockery. This builds grudges inside you against your family members.

Looking at some other acts, you wish to hang out with some female friends or you wish to invite them home but you're afraid that your wife may strongly disapprove. Hence you may end up not doing so and you may hold grudges against her. You may wish to interact with them through social media platforms but you're afraid that your wife may create a scene if she finds out. Hence you may abstain from doing so and you may hold grudges against her.

You wish to make a career in sports, singing, acting or some other field but you're afraid that your parents will not allow it, as they want you to study a lot and become a doctor or engineer. You wish to marry a girl you love but you're afraid that your family will stand in strong opposition to this marriage as she belongs to a different religion. You're suffering in marriage but you can't move out of it as your family pressurizes you to make it work. You wish to try non-vegetarian food but you're afraid your family will disapprove strongly since it is a traditional vegetarian family.

Such incidents as well as other likewise incidents may build grudges and regrets inside you. As a result, you may start disliking people who you think are responsible for not letting you do many things that you want to do. At the same time, you may start disliking a part of yourself for not standing up to what you believe in. With time and more incidents, the number of grudges may increase and it may start causing potential damage to your relationships.

Let's see how this problem may be fixed. In most cases, two types of restrictions imposed on you cause grudges. The first one is imposed by your family and/or other people. The second type is imposed by yourself, under pretext of a number of fears. For example, you may choose not to wear a dress because you're afraid that people will disapprove or mock you. In this case, you're imposing a restriction on yourself since the opinion of people matters more to you than your own freewill. No one is actually stopping you from wearing this dress and you're choosing not to wear it as you can't handle people's disapproval or mockery.

Looking at another example, suppose you wish to make a career in some sport. However, your parents disapprove and they force you to make a career in medical science. You succumb to the pressure and you unwillingly pursue medical science. This builds grudges which are of the first type. You wish to do something and you're prepared to take chances. Hence you're not abstaining on account of what other people may think. Your family is putting pressure on you and you can't handle this pressure. Hence in this case, a major share of such restriction has been put on you by your family.

At first, you should learn to differentiate between these two types of restrictions. The ones that you put on yourself are relatively easy to handle. Hence it's better to start with them. As always, start with small activities and then build up. For example, if you want to wear a pair of worn-out jeans, start doing so without bothering about what people may think or how they may react. Some people may disapprove but that doesn't matter, as it is your and not their choice to make. You've achieved two goals by doing so. You've worn a pair of jeans you like and you've taken care of a grudge.

Some people may like how you look and they may approve. Such approvals may give you good feeling and more than that, this experience may teach you an important lesson. Whatever you do, some people may approve and some may disapprove. They're doing their jobs and you should do yours. It means you should do what you think is right for you and you should not bother about what people think or how they react.

In the beginning, focus more on approvals and try to ignore disapprovals. Once you reach advance stages, you should ignore disapprovals as well as approvals. This is because even in case of approvals, the evaluation of your actions as well as that of you is dependent on the opinions of people and not on you. The validation of your actions as well as your personality should come from within and not from outside, as that is the only way for true validation. This is why spiritually advanced people may do what they feel is right and they may not care about how other people judge them.

However in the beginning, it is better to get approvals from people. Hence focus on the approvals. Likewise, start engaging in similar type of activities which are somewhat difficult at this level but not a lot more difficult. Once you're comfortable with this level, you should move to the next one. At this level, try activities which are somewhat more difficult than those in the first level. However, they should not be a lot more difficult.

This way, you can replace the script on your subconscious with time and efforts. As you engage in more and more things that you wish to do, the number of grudges may drop. As that happens, you may feel more relaxed and much more positive, since a lot of negativity has left you along with the grudges that you had for so long. Once you reach advance stages, start doing what you feel is right in every sphere of life, even if it upsets your family members. With time, they'll learn to respect your decisions or they'll learn to accommodate.

Be wise enough to stay away from practices which may pose actual problems for other people, even if you wish to engage in them. For example, you may wish to drink a lot on regular basis. However, you can't handle alcohol beyond a point. Hence whenever you have a lot of it, you fight with your family members, spouse, friends and/or other people. You often put others in difficulties after consuming a lot of alcohol. In this case, you should stay away from alcohol unless you can learn to control the quantity of alcohol you consume. Though you may feel like having alcohol, you should not.

You're free to do whatever you like as long as it doesn't pose real problems for others. If it does, it's not your individual choice to make and it becomes a collective choice. On the other hand, if you consume alcohol in decent quantities and you never cause problems for others after drinking; consuming alcohol is fine for you. In case a family member has an issue with it; it is not a real issue and it is his imaginary problem. Hence he should learn to deal with it and you should not restrict yourself.

As long as an action of yours doesn't cause real problems for other people, you have the right to engage in such action on your own, without taking approvals from others. However, if an action of yours affects other people, it needs their approval. Taking another example, suppose you wish to smoke in a room where five other people are present and all of them strongly object as they also have to breathe in toxins they don't wish to. Hence it is not your individual decision. If everyone in the room is comfortable with you smoking, you may do so. Otherwise, get out of the room, smoke and get back.

Looking at this equation from a different angle, if these people are your family members and some of them disapprove even if you go outside and smoke, as they don't want you to smoke, it is not a real problem. Hence you're free to make your choice without caring for their approvals. The same rule applies to all other spheres.

Whenever your actions affect other people in reality, their approvals or disapprovals matter. If your actions don't cause real problems for them and they have imaginary issues which means they are against your actions without valid reasons, their approvals or disapprovals don't matter. Hence be wise enough to know which actions of yours are the ones which don't need approvals from other people. Start doing more and more such things which you wish to do but you've held yourself back so far, due to fear of disapproval from others.

Looking at the other type of restriction, it is more difficult to handle. This is because other people are a part of it and you alone are not responsible for everything. In this case, if you feel that you're right in doing whatever you wish to do and your dear ones should not make one such decision for you, try to convince them. An effective way of doing so is by seeking help from someone in your circle, who is wise and who is valued by such dear ones in question.

A wise man may not only understand that what you wish to do is right for you, he may also be able to convince your dear ones to understand your point of view. It means you should always keep company with wise people as they may resolve a number of your problems without much trouble or effort. Apart from that, you may try to convince your dear ones by yourself, if you're good at doing so.

If you don't have one such wise person in your circle and you fail to convince your people on your own, a grudge may be created in this case, since you may not wish to go against your people. Though you may not stop this grudge from building, you may do things to reduce the damage it may cause. Firstly, try to reduce the overall number of grudges that you have. If you're able to get rid of majority of your grudges, the remaining ones may become much easier to handle.

Secondly, you should help other people who may be in similar situations. For example, if someone's parents are stopping him from doing something that he wishes to do and which may be a right thing to do, you can try to convince his parents to let him do so. If you're able to convince his parents and they let him do what he wishes, you may feel that the similar grudge within you has lost a lot of strength. Through his person, you may see yourself doing what he wishes to do. This may provide relief.

This is why you may have seen in some movies that a character tends to help many people stuck in situations, which he might have faced and suffered from. As he helps them get out of such situations, he feels relived as if he's got himself out of one such situation. Hence trying to help other people do what you can't do may reduce the strength of similar types of grudges within you.

Looking at another approach to handle such situations, you may choose to engage in certain actions which you feel are right, despite strong opposition from your loved ones. If you take this path, you may offend some of your loved ones and at times, the damage may be serious. Hence this option should be the last one. It should be used only in cases when what you want to do is of utmost importance to you but your family or loved ones are standing in opposition to it.

During one such moment, you have to take loss one way or the other. You'll either end up quitting something that holds utmost value to you or you may end up causing serious damage to a relationship. Which one of these losses you want to take is dependent on your personality type, priorities and a number of other factors.

As long as you're social and you're living in the concept of family; there'll always be compromises that you'll need to make. Family and friends do a lot for you and being humans; they may expect a lot from you in return. At times, their expectations may make perfect sense whereas at times, they may be completely nonsense. Even in the latter case, you may not always have the luxury to reject their choices or opinions; and you may have to honour their expectations despite knowing they're wrong.

This is necessary evil and there's not much you can do about it, as long as you're living in one such concept. Only a person living alone may make all his choices on his own. However in that case, he may miss out on a number of beautiful and meaningful things which family and loved ones may add to life. Hence for a person living in society, a balance needs to be struck. Follow all such choices of yours which are right and which may not offend your loved ones a lot. Though they may still offend them somewhat, such damage is easily repaired in most cases, since families are bound by strong bonds and they're not shaken by small things.

Whenever you feel that a choice of yours may cause serious damage to a relationship; you have to pursue or leave such choice after carefully assessing what matters more for you. If such relationship matters more, leave the choice and be prepared to handle a grudge. If the choice matters more, follow it and be prepared to handle a potentially troubled relationship.

By engaging in aforementioned practices, you may reduce the number of grudges and you may also reduce the quantum of grudges which can't be avoided. Always start with small activities and build up from there. Never attempt such tasks at any level, which may be a lot more difficult compared to what you can handle at such level.

Too Much Work

In the first part of this book, we discussed the habit of laziness and now we're going to discuss the habit of working too much. These two habits have their roots in the same cause and they are two extreme expressions of one problem. It is the problem of not being able to strike balance between work and rest.

If you're resting much more than you should and you're working less or much less than you should; you're lazy. However, if you're working much more than you should and you're relaxing less or much less than you should, you're working too much. In both the cases, you're missing the element of balance which is an important element for each and every habit/trait as well as sphere of life.

For instance, if you eat much less than you should or you eat much more than you should, you may face health issues. Likewise, if you spend too much time with your family and you don't give much time to your profession or you give too much time to profession and you don't have time for personal affairs, you may face problems. Balance is required in each and every sphere of life and whenever such balance is disturbed, it may cause broadly two types of problems lying on the opposite extremes.

For instance, your body temperature may drop or it may go up whenever there is some issue which it can't handle. As long as it is balanced, the temperature may stay within normal range. Likewise, the weather may become problematic when it is too hot or too cold and it seems to work best when it is within normal temperature zones. The same applies to all other spheres.

Hence if you work too much and you take little rest and/or you have little time to attend to your personal affairs, you may end up causing problems in your personal life and/or health problems. Though you may think that by working too much you may achieve success earlier and the quantum of such success may be more, it may not be so in reality.

In order to understand this concept in proper manner, let's first try to find out proper definition of success. Common definition of success says 'accomplishment of an aim'. However, this definition is incomplete as it lacks important information. A better definition of success is 'accomplishment of an aim minus the cost you have paid to accomplish such aim'. Such cost may be in form of money, efforts, health, peace, relationships and other things.

It means the net amount of success is calculated by subtracting the cost from the overall value of what you have achieved. Hence if various people achieve the same objective but they pay different costs, their successes are not same and they're different.

Let's take an example to understand this concept in a better manner. Suppose you sell a product for 100 dollars. Your net profit will be calculated after deducting the purchase cost of this product plus the expenses you incurred to sell this product. If you purchased this product for 80 dollars and 10 dollars were spent towards the expenses, the total cost of this product is 90 dollars and you sell it for 100 dollars, which means a profit of 10 dollars.

However if someone else sells the same product for 100 dollars when his purchase cost is 80 dollars and overhead expenses are 25 dollars, he will not get any profit in this case. The total of purchase price and overhead expenses for this product is 105 dollars in this case and he sells it for 100 dollars. This means that the second person is facing a loss of 5 dollars and not a profit of 10 dollars unlike the first person, though both of them have sold the same product for the same amount.

Likewise, a third person may witness a profit of 5 dollars, a fourth one may witness a profit of 20 dollars and another one may witness a loss of 10 dollars by selling the same product for the same price, depending on the total of purchase cost plus overheads. Though everyone is selling the same product for the same price and the resultant success seems to be the same from distance, everyone's success is different and some of them are even facing losses. Hence the net amount of success is not what you have achieved but it is what you have achieved, minus what you have invested or what you have lost in order to achieve such success.

Let's look at this example from a different angle to understand more about this concept. Let's consider it from buyer's point of view. Suppose a person buys this product for 100 dollars from a shop close to his house. Another person buys it from an online store which charges 4 dollars for shipping apart from 100 dollars as the cost of this product. Yet another person purchases the same product online with 100 dollars as the cost of this product and 7 dollars as shipping charges. Though all of them have purchased the same product, the overall cost of this product is different for them.

Hence the net amount of success you achieve in any sphere of your life is calculated after deducting the resources spent and losses taken, from it. Therefore it should be kept in mind that a particular success may hold good value for you, only if the net amount of resources spent and losses taken to achieve such success is less or far less than the value delivered by such success. On the other hand, if you have spent more resources and taken more losses to achieve a particular objective than the value delivered by such objective, the net equation does not correspond to success but it corresponds to loss.

Let's look at an example from the life of someone I know. This person has been working with a company for many years. He has been working day and night to achieve top position in this company and in order to do so, he has been ignoring all other spheres of his life for many years, as his eyes are focused on his target. This person has recently become vice-president in this company. There is another person working for the same company who started working for the company about a year before the first person did. The second person is still holding a rank lower than the vice-president.

Looking from distance, the first person obviously seems to have achieved more success than the second one and it seems that his habit of working a lot has paid off. However, this equation may change when we dig deep into the actual amount of success achieved by these two people.

The first person has already had two divorces and the primary reason for both these divorces was that he gave little time to his wives. At times, he ignored them altogether even when they needed him very much. Whenever his wives asked for his attention or presence for some important affairs, he was busy with work and so he made excuses and ignored them. He kept working overtime and late nights in order to achieve top position in his company. After many years of working too much, he did achieve his target or so to say, he became successful.

However, this success has cost him two broken marriages and he is alone at this time. Apart from that, he is facing some health issues which have appeared due to his habit of working too much and in doing so, not eating properly and not taking proper rest. He has also developed a habit of drinking a lot which according to him is a good way of getting rid of his loneliness and bitter memories of his two marriages. He now misses his first wife a lot, he regrets his decision of not giving her proper attention and care, and he wishes he could do something to fix certain broken things.

Though the second person has achieved less amount of visible success than the first person, he is having a good marriage and he is blessed with a loving wife and two lovely kids. Though this person devoted the required amount of effort and time to his job, he knew the value of family, health and other important aspects of life. Hence he didn't want to sacrifice any of these aspects in order to achieve more success in his profession. So he did his job with honesty and that honesty got him many promotions. However, he gave due time and attention to his wife, family, health and enjoyment also. As a result, he is a happy man with a good marriage, good health and a positive mindset.

You see, though the first person seems to have achieved more at the first glance, it turns out that the second person is indeed more successful as he has not paid any unwanted cost to achieve success and he has also not taken any losses to achieve success. On the other hand, the first person has invested much more to achieve somewhat more success and he has also taken big losses on the front of his marriage, family, health and mindset. His mindset has now become negative and he has started questioning the value of his success which was what he wanted the most at a time.

Hence the second person has achieved good amount of net success whereas the first person has taken losses which have value far greater than the value of the success he has achieved. Therefore, the cost to be paid for a particular success must be assessed before working towards that success, as the cost paid may be higher or much higher than the value delivered by that particular success.

After establishing a better definition of success, let's move on to the habit of working too much. People suffering from this problem usually work too much in order to achieve one kind of professional success or another. In doing so, they may not pay required attention to other important spheres of their lives. This practice creates problems in other spheres of their lives. Though they may witness good results in their professions, they may suffer on other important fronts of their lives. When that happens, the overall quality of their lives may go down, the impact of which may start reflecting on their professions also, in many cases.

Hence you need to assign due importance to relaxation, personal affairs and other important affairs, in order to lead a balanced life. When you keep ignoring most other spheres in pursuit of professional success; your conscious mind sends messages to the subconscious that professional success is the most important objective for you and you're willing to ignore/sacrifice anything in order to achieve it. With repeated messages, a script is written on your subconscious. When that happens, it encourages you to ignore everything else and focus on professional success only.

It means you've now developed a natural tendency to ignore most spheres of your life and you don't need to consciously work for this. Hence you may naturally start ignoring important tasks from most other spheres in order to devote most of your time and efforts to professional success. This may continue for years and by the time you realize how much cost you've paid, much damage may have been done, some of which may be irreversible.

Profession is an important sphere of life but excess of everything is bad. Proper rest and due relaxation are important to keep you healthy, both physically as well as mentally. Therefore, you should take due rest and relax yourself whenever it is needed. You may have noticed that when the players of a football team or cricket team play too many matches in a relatively short period of time, their performances drop and they start losing matches. This is because their schedules demand them to work too much and such overwork takes a toll on them. They are not able to rest and relax as much as they need, in order to maintain optimum levels of performances.

Accordingly, their performances starts dropping and as a result, they start losing more matches than they usually do. Some of these players may even go on record and say that they have been playing too much in the recent times due to which their performances have dropped and they need a break to relax and hit the game again, with their strengths restored.

We use mobile phones and various other gadgets which draw energy from their batteries. In order for these gadgets to keep performing, their batteries must be recharged at regular intervals. Otherwise, their batteries may lose all their power and stop supplying energy to the gadgets. As a result, the gadgets will stop working.

Similarly, the cars we drive need fuel, maintenance and rest at regular intervals in order to perform properly. If any of these ingredients is missing, our cars may either not perform properly or they may not perform at all.

Just like the gadgets and cars, all other things and entities need due amount of rest/relaxation in order to perform properly. Same is the case with humans and we also need due amount of rest and relaxation at regular intervals in order to keep performing properly. Ignoring due amount of rest/ relaxation and working too much may start decreasing your performance like a car which has not been maintained properly for a long period of time. Hence you should have due amount of rest/ relaxation in order to recharge yourself and keep performing properly.

Other problems with working too much are that you may tend to ignore your family members as well as your health since you keep yourself busy with work most of the time. This may create problems in your family and as a result, you may have to witness heated arguments, frequent fights, no communication for long periods of time and in the worst case, you may have to suffer the loss of an entire relationship.

Paying too much attention to professional work and ignoring life partner is one of the primary reasons which cause so many divorces in this day and age. People are giving so much time and attention to their professions that they keep ignoring the needs of their life partners. Hence one such person may achieve more professional success but he may pay high prices for such success. The institution of marriage demands time, care and attention from both partners in order to be healthy. Too much focus on work may significantly reduce the amount of time, care and attention you may give you to your partner. As a result, you marriage may suffer or fail.

At times, it happens that both the partners are working and one of them receives an opportunity for promotion with transfer to another city or state. The partner who's been offered such promotion or a better job opportunity in a faraway city wants the other partner to move whereas the other partner doesn't want to move as doing so hurts his/her professional growth.

This is a situation where one of the two partners has to take a professional loss or make a professional compromise in order to keep having a happy marriage. However, none of them may be willing to make a compromise or take a loss and they may both expect the other one to make such compromise or take such loss. Isn't it strange that we demand our partners to make such compromises when we're ourselves not ready to make them?

At times, one partner may unwillingly take a loss and move with the other partner. When that happens, such partner may build grudges against the other partner. Such grudges may deteriorate the quality of marriage. At other times, none of them may be willing to make such compromise and the marriage may collapse due to this issue. The marriage fails because both the partners have become so obsessed with their professions that they are willing to take any losses in order to achieve more professional success.

Profession is a part of your life and it is not your entire life. Accordingly, you should pay due attention to other spheres of your life along with paying due attention to your profession. Happiness lies in a balanced mix of everything from each sphere of life and too much of anything may ruin it in most cases. Hence take a balanced approach towards life and stop letting your work ruin your personal life, health and other important spheres.

In order to treat the problem of too much work, start maintaining a schedule for your work as well as other spheres. For example, if you have a job where the working hours are 10 hours a day and five days a week, make sure that you don't do your professional work apart from those 10 hours a day on weekdays. Stop doing overtime and especially stop bringing home your office work as doing so may seriously disturb your family life.

This is because no husband, wife or kids want you to be the office guy when you are at home with them, after working long hours at the office. Use this time to relax yourself, take some rest and spend some time with your family members or friends so that you may attend to some of their needs, which may strengthen your relationships with them. You should work overtime or bring office work home; only in case of emergencies or other situations which so demand. It's fine if you need to do so once in a while since you owe that much to your profession. However, don't make a habit of it.

The days when you don't have to go to your office like weekly holidays, plan them in a way that you are able to spend this time partly in relaxing, resting and entertaining yourself, and partly in attending to the needs and demands of your family members. For example, if your wife and kids want you to take them to a movie and a dinner afterwards, don't keep yourself busy with work on such days and instead do what they wish.

Likewise, you can read a book, surf on internet, watch a movie or some other TV program, go for swimming, help your wife with some domestic tasks, listen to her and help her make decisions on some family matters or matters related to her profession, play with your kids, help them in studies, hang out with friends and do many other such things which are the keys to a happy life.

Professional success can give you more resources. More resources may help you enjoy more and have a better life. However in order to do so, you must devote due time for such better quality of life. Most professional institutes work 5 or 6 days a week and they take breaks for 1 or 2 days every weak. This is because they understand that their employees need to relax and do a number of other tasks related to various spheres of their lives. Hence they offer breaks so that the employees may relax and recover from the workload. When that happens, the employees are able to perform properly for years and years. Hence don't use your days off for work and use them for personal spheres.

Some people fix some targets and they think they'll start enjoying once they reach such targets. What they may not realize is that by working so much; they've written scripts on their subconscious minds and these scripts feature no enjoyment. Hence they may not be able to relax/enjoy even when they achieve such targets. They may naturally (subconsciously) set new targets and they may think they'll enjoy once they achieve those targets. This may continue and they may never enjoy.

Like many other things, the ability to relax and enjoy also works like a habit. If you have this habit, you may be able to enjoy and relax. If you don't have this habit, you may not be able to enjoy and relax; even if you have all the resources and time. Hence along with the habit of working, you need to develop the habit of relaxing and enjoying, in order to maintain balance between work and relaxation.

Too Much Complaining

This habit is a branch of the habit of negative attitude and it writes a specific type of negative pattern on the subconscious mind. Due to this pattern, people suffering from this habit can't help complaining about most people, situations and things they come across.

Let's look at some common expressions of people having this habit. They are; the tea is too hot or the tea is not as hot as it should be; the coffee is too strong or the coffee is too light; the water is not cold enough or the water is too cold to drink; this food item has not been cooked properly or it has been overcooked; this bread is not as soft as it should be or this bread is a little too soft; and this dress is a little too short or it is a little too long.

Moving on, this sofa is a little too comfortable or this sofa is not as comfortable as it should be; the paint on this wall is a little too dark or the paint is not as dark as it should be; this movie is not as romantic as it should be or this movie is a little too romantic; that character in the movie is not as expressive as it should be or that character is a little too expressive; the caramel popcorns don't have enough caramel on them or they have too much caramel on them.

Likewise; this gym has fewer treadmills or the gym has too many treadmills; the air conditioning is a little too effective or it is not as effective as it should be, which means either the temperature is a little too low or it is not as low as it should be; that trainer does not have as much muscle as a trainer should have or that trainer is too muscular; the airplane fare should include meals (when the fare is cheap) or the fare should be less (when it includes meals); you are driving fast or you are driving slow; the speech was too short or the speech was too long; you are calling a little too early or you are calling a little too late; you pay too little attention to my needs or you interfere too much with my affairs; you don't have any emotions or you are too emotional; you are not mature enough for me or you are too mature for me; and many other such complaints.

It is interesting to note that in most of these cases, the person complaining has a reason to complain in situations which are opposite to each other. For example, if one such person is your wife and you decide to take interest in many of her day to day affairs in order to show love and concern, you may hear from her that you are interfering too much with her affairs and you should give her more space as you are restricting her freedom. On the other hand, when you start doing that and you start giving her more space by not interfering in most of her day to day affairs, she may have another complaint. She may say that you don't care for her any longer and that is why you don't take interest in most of her day to day activities.

Similarly if one such person is your husband and you like dressing up most of the time, he may complain that you look too formal most of the time and you should avoid doing so, as there is no need for it. On the other hand, if you don't believe in dressing up and you like dressing easy and comfortable most of the time, he may complain that your dressing manner is way too boring most of the time and you should dress better. The point is that no matter which way you may choose to behave or do certain things, people suffering from this negative habit will always find ways to complain.

It should be noted that each one of us has his own tastes and choices when it comes to certain things and there are no problems with having such choices. For example, someone may have a taste for having his tea or coffee served very hot and he may complain whenever it is less than very hot, though another person may find it fairly hot. Similarly, someone may like the air conditioning set to very high as he feels more comfortable with low temperatures and accordingly he may complain if the air conditioning is set to normal, though that normal may be reasonably good for many people.

Having such specific choices in a some spheres of your life and even in many spheres of your life does not make you have the habit of complaining too much, as you are simply trying to get things done according to your liking and nothing else. The difference between a person having this problem and the one not having it is that in case of first one of the aforementioned examples, the person having this habit may complain if tea is not very hot as well as if it is very hot. On the other hand, a normal person may complain when tea is not very hot but he may complement when tea is very hot. This is because he has got what he likes and so he pays complement to the one who has made it.

Similarly in case of second example, the person suffering from this habit may complain if the air conditioning is set to low temperature as well as if the air conditioning is set to high or even normal temperature. On the other hand, the person not having this problem may complain when the air conditioning is set to normal or higher temperature but he may feel happy and he may pay complement when the air conditioning is set to low temperature as this is what he likes.

Hence the difference between having specific choices and having a problem of complaining too much is that the first type of people may complain when they don't get what they like and they may complement when they get what they like. On the other hand, the second type of people may find reasons to complain in almost any type of situation. Hence the first type of people want their likings to be done and they are happy when their choices are met whereas the second type of people simply want to find ways to complain in most cases.

Therefore, if you can complain and complement in a good ratio, you are not suffering from this problem and you only want certain things to be done according to your liking. There is nothing wrong with that, unless you want things which are too difficult for other people to arrange or manage, in most cases. On the other hand, if you hardly complement people or situations even when they are according to your liking and you tend to find ways to complain in most situations, which means that the percentage of complaints made by you is much higher than the percentage of complements given by you, you are suffering from the problem of complaining too much.

Let's try to understand the cause of this habit. In order to understand it in the best possible way, let's first try to understand as to when do people complain? Most people complain when they are not getting what they like and instead they are getting something they don't like, which makes these people dissatisfied and hence they complain. So the key factor working behind a complaint is dissatisfaction whereas that in case of a complement is satisfaction in most cases. People tend to complement when they are satisfied with what they are getting and they tend to complain when they are dissatisfied with what they are getting.

Hence dissatisfaction lies in the root of complaints as you may complain when you are dissatisfied. It may not become a problem as long as you also have the habit of giving complements when you are satisfied. Since people suffering from this negative habit tend to complain in most situations and they hardly complement anyone or anything, and since all the complaints come from dissatisfactions, it means that such people have developed a habit of being dissatisfied with most situations, things and people. Due to this habit, they feel dissatisfied in most situations and that is why they complain.

Such people have written the script of being dissatisfied in most situations, on their subconscious minds. This script can be written due to more than one reason. Looking at one such reason, a person suffering from this habit has gone through a long series of events which were dissatisfying, in the early years of this life or for a long period of time in his past life. These conscious experiences wrote a script on his mind that most people, things and situations are not going to bring anything good to him and instead they are going to do one bad thing or another to him. Accordingly, his subconscious mind starts finding reasons for dissatisfaction in most situations, since it is convinced that such situations will end up in dissatisfaction.

To understand this reason with the help of real life examples, let's take a close look into the childhood of a person suffering from this problem. As a child, this person kept facing situation after situation for many years, where all these situations brought bad things or bad results to him due to which he was hurt and dissatisfied. For example, he did not have sufficient to eat many times during his childhood. Whenever it was the time for a meal, he knew that he was not going to be satisfied with food as it was not going to be enough. All the times he was dissatisfied due to lack of proper food, these conscious acts of dissatisfaction sent messages to his subconscious mind that food was supposed to dissatisfy.

Likewise, whenever this child wanted to wear clothes, he didn't have good clothes most of the time and he had to make do with whatever was available which was far below the mark in most cases, and which caused dissatisfaction again and again. Through all these conscious acts of dissatisfaction while wearing clothes, messages were conveyed to his subconscious mind that wearing clothes is what causes dissatisfaction. All the while this child ate his food again and again, and he wore bad clothes again and again, he kept complaining about such food and clothes. These continuous and conscious complaints wrote a script of dissatisfaction for food and clothes.

Similarly, this child had to suffer a lot due to lack of resources in many spheres of his life or due to other reasons. Hence he felt dissatisfied many times and he made conscious complaints many times. Whether it was being sent to a bad school; not having all the required books and stationary; no pocket money or little pocket money most of the time; little enjoyment or entertainment like going out for holidays or picnics; being ignored by parents due to most of the attention going to another sibling; being ignored or undervalued by schoolmates and playmates while taking part in studies and sports; having used cycle, scooter and other vehicles as the new ones were given to elder siblings; wearing old clothes and shoes which were already worn by an elder sibling and many other such reasons, all of them made this child feel dissatisfied and complain again and again.

Such conscious dissatisfactions and complaints towards most spheres of his life kept sending more and more messages to his subconscious mind that no matter what the circumstances or the situations might be, he was only going to be dissatisfied in the end. Such great number of conscious messages wrote a script of dissatisfaction and complaints on his subconscious mind. Accordingly, he started apprehending that most situations were only going to bring dissatisfaction to him and he would only end up suffering in most situations. As this script becomes stronger and stronger, this child starts finding reasons to feel dissatisfied and complain in most situations because this is what he apprehends, is going to happen to him.

Gradually this child grows old. Though he may not consciously know the root cause of his problem, or even the problem itself, he has developed a habit of feeling dissatisfied and making complaints in most situations. It may seem strange to some people why this person is finding one reason or another to make complaints about some food item when that item is good. It may not be that strange if you look into the subconscious script of this person. He has been finding dissatisfaction in food for a long period of time, which wrote a subconscious script that food brings dissatisfaction. Though the limited quantity of food or the bad taste of the food suffered by him is gone now, the habit of feeling dissatisfied with food has not gone.

Hence he tends to find one fault or another with food because he has a subconscious habit of finding fault with food items. Though the faults may not be there, the habit is there. Similarly, he may find faults with most clothing items and complain about them as his subconscious dissatisfaction with clothes is strong. Though the clothes may be good now, this habit makes him find some faults and complain about clothes. Likewise, his behavior of complaints in most other spheres of his life can be explained on similar basis.

It should be noted that this person has to have a weak and overall negative personality in order to suffer from this habit, and this weakness and negativity accompanies him right from his childhood or even from his previous life. This is due to the reason that if this person was strong and positive as a child, though he might have faced many of the above mentioned trouble causing situations during his childhood, his reactions towards these problems, final interpretations of such situations and the messages sent by him to his subconscious mind would have been different than they were in case of a child with weak and negative personality.

This means that a strong and positive child would not have suffered in many such situations and he would have sent different messages to his subconscious mind. For example, this child would either have refused to wear used clothes or shoes retired by his elder siblings and he would have strongly demanded for these items to be new; or he would not have bothered much about wearing such used items and he would have been happy with them. In both these cases, the child would have ended up in a situation where he was not left dissatisfied as in the first case, he got what he wanted and in the second case, he liked what he got. So there is no place for dissatisfaction and accordingly there is no place for complaints.

Hence the messages sent to the subconscious mind by this type of child were not negative ones but they were positive ones. The first type of messages said that he would not settle for something he didn't like and the second type of messages said that he was willing to enjoy what he had instead of crying over what he could not have. Similarly, this child would not have allowed his schoolmates and friends to ignore him as he was strong and he knew how to make his own place among people and more than that, how to make people respect him and follow him.

In the same way, this child would have found ways to feel satisfied and happy, in most of the other aforementioned seemingly bad situations. Accordingly, he would not have developed the habit of complaining too much as he didn't feel dissatisfied many times during his childhood. On the contrary, this child is likely to develop into a person who is positive and strong enough to change many of the seemingly unfavorable situations to his favor and make the most of these situations even when there is nothing much these situations can offer.

This is because this person has put up many fights against the situations he didn't like and he has won many of these fights by gaining through many of these situations. Because of that, he has developed a subconscious habit of not being bothered by unfavorable situations as he knows how to make the most of these situations.

Therefore, it is the weak and negative child who is likely to suffer from this problem because he does not have either of the two gifts that a strong and positive child has. He can't take a stand against things and situations he doesn't like since he is not strong enough to put up a fight and win. He is not positive enough to enjoy whatever he is getting instead of crying for what he wants. Hence weakness and negativity must be a part of the personality of this person in order for him to suffer from this problem, as a strong and positive person is good enough not to feel dissatisfied in most situations.

Another reasons for making too many complaints is being overambitious. Being overambitious is one negative trait which can make you feel dissatisfied in most situations, with most things and with most people. People complaining too much due to being overambitious are different from the already discussed type of people having this problem. Unlike the first type of people suffering from this problem, these people actually may not suffer much or suffer at all in many situations. All their dissatisfaction and complaints are due to the fact that they have a habit of wanting more and more.

No matter how good a thing, situation or a person may be, one such person may still not feel satisfied as the ideal image of this thing, situation or person in his mind is too big, too great and too perfect to be true. No matter how good his job is, it is still nothing compared to his dream job; no matter how good his girlfriend is, she is still nothing compared to his perfect dream girlfriend; no matter how well his son performs at studies, he is still far behind his dream target; and no matter how good the food or hospitality is at a place, it is still nothing compared to his ideal definition of food and hospitality.

Likewise, no matter how well behaved a person is, he is still nothing compared to his ideal image of a well behaved person; no matter how luxurious a car may be, it still lacks something compared to the luxuries offered by his dream car; and many other such examples of many other such situations where there's nothing wrong with a thing or a person. However one such person may still not feel satisfied as he has raised his expectations too high.

It's not a bad thing to demand for better things when the things being offered are not good enough. Likewise, there's nothing wrong in trying to raise your standards on all levels, as long as all this remains reasonable which is exactly what is not the case with a person suffering from the problem of being overambitious. One such person raises the level of his expectations, ambitions and demands so high that it may be almost impossible for most people and situations to meet such expectations. Inevitably, dissatisfaction and complaints follow in most situations as it is almost impossible to make this person happy and satisfied. Hence the negative habit of being overambitious can make you have the negative habit of complaining too much also.

Looking at another reason, people suffering from inferiority complex as well as negative mindset may have this problem. Due to a combination of these traits, they complain about most people, things and situations. By doing so, they're trying to make most people, things and situations small so that they may feel bigger in comparison. When most people around them have a number of flaws (according to the people suffering from this habit), it makes them feel better in comparison. Hence they try to belittle people and things in order to feel bigger and better.

Let's look at some remedies which may help you get rid of this habit if you have it. Since various people may have his habit due to different reasons, you need to find your reason first, in order to implement appropriate remedies. For example, if you have this habit because of low confidence as well as negative mindset, which is the third case; you need to treat these two habits and your problem of complaining too much may go away.

If you have a weak and/or negative personality and you have gone through a troubled childhood where you suffered many times due to lack of one thing or another, you are having this habit due to the first reason. If you didn't have a troubled childhood and you don't have a weak personality but you have big dreams, you aspire to rise sky high, you want most people and things to be perfect and nothing less than perfect; and you always have some better idea for a situation, you're overambitious.

If you suffer from this problem due to being overambitious, all you have to do is treat your problem of being overambitious and the problem of complaining too much will also go away with that.

Coming to the last reason, if you are suffering from this problem due to a weak and negative personality, as well as due to a troubled childhood, your path of treatment is going to be long or very long. In order to get rid of this problem in this case, you will first need to work towards building a stronger personality so that you may be able to fight and change situations which you don't like, instead of keeping quiet and complaining later on. For this, learn to handle lack of confidence and lack of courage.

Apart from that, you will also need to reduce the overall negativity in your aura/personality so that you may become able to appreciate and make the most of what you have instead of complaining about what you want to have but don't have. In order to reduce the overall negativity of your personality, you should take guidance from this part as well as from the first part of this book. You should try to rectify or reduce as many negative habits as many you can so that you may finally have a positive aura or positive personality which can not only help you get rid of this negative habit, but many other negative habits too.

Let's look at some conscious activities which may help you get rid of this habit due to the reason being discussed. These activities may provide extra help and the primary way to fix this problem is by taking care of your weak and negative personality. Looking at these specific activities, though you can't like what you get if you don't want it, you can certainly try and get many small things that you really like and then appreciate them. Doing so through conscious activities again and again, will send more and more messages to your subconscious mind.

All these messages will say that you can feel satisfied and you can appreciate also, instead of feeling dissatisfied and making complaints all the time. As the number of these messages sent through your specifically targeted conscious activities increases, you subconscious mind will start adjusting to the new script.

In order to do so, you have to choose activities which you really like and which are small so that you don't have problems engaging in them and completing them. These acts have to be conscious as engaging in conscious acts is the best way to see better results at the earliest. At the first level, you should choose small conscious activities like going to a restaurant or some food joint which offers some of your favorite food items and the taste is just what you like the most. It doesn't have to be a major meal and it could be something small like a snack.

Take this food item and try to eat and enjoy it as consciously as you can. It means you should not attend to any phone calls, talk to anyone else or look at some TV screen while having this food item and you should devote your entire concentration to eating and enjoying this food item. Finish this food item by enjoying it to the maximum and after that, complement the management or the chef whichever is possible, for serving you with such a tasty food item. Since you really like this food item and you have enjoyed it, it will be comparatively easy for you to feel satisfied and give complement. This feeling of satisfaction and the act of giving complement send signals to your subconscious mind that you can enjoy and complement also.

Similarly choose from other small items like sweets, chocolates, potato chips, ice creams, juices, soft drinks and many other such items which you really like a lot. Eat or drink them with your entire focus on enjoying them, feel satisfied and then tell any person near you that you ate or drank this item and you really loved it. For example, eat a small pack of your favorite brand and flavor of chocolate with conscious focus. Once it is finished, tell your friend, colleague, girlfriend or anyone else near you that you really love this brand as well as flavor of chocolate and you enjoy it a lot. Once again, you have sent message to your subconscious mind, through this specifically targeted conscious activity that you can enjoy and complement.

In order to engage in more conscious, small and specific activities of the same type, you can choose to listen to or watch your favorite songs with conscious focus; watch some of your favorite scenes from some movies; read a few lines from your favorite books or articles; put on your favorite perfumes and enjoy them; talk to your favorite people and enjoy the conversation; get together with your favorite people and enjoy this get together to the maximum; play your favorite video games, computer games or any other types of games and enjoy them thoroughly; wear your favorite dresses again and again in rotation and enjoy wearing them; engage in your favorite hobbies and enjoy doing so, like swimming, playing football, shopping, watching movies and other such hobbies; and engage in many other such activities which you like a lot.

While engaging in these activities, you should make sure that such activities meet some compulsory conditions as otherwise, the purpose of engaging in them may not be served. At the first level, the activities must be the ones you really like engaging in. You must engage in them consciously which means devoting your entire concentration to these activities by not doing anything else simultaneously. You must enjoy, feel satisfied and give complement to someone after that. If anyone of these compulsory things is missing, you may not be able to witness proper benefits.

Therefore, after listening to your favorite song and enjoying it, you must tell someone that you really like listening to this song and it makes you happy. Follow the same pattern in case of other such activities by concentrating on them, enjoying them to the fullest and by saying good words about those activities to someone else. The most important part of this remedy is to enjoy an activity to the fullest and then say good words about it. These two acts when done consciously, will send messages to your subconscious mind that you can enjoy and pay complements.

If you engage in an activity but you don't enjoy it consciously like drinking your favorite mango juice while talking to someone else, a strong message of 'I can enjoy' won't be sent to your subconscious mind. This is because you did not enjoy the juice actively and you just drank it passively while you were talking to someone else. Similarly, when you enjoy drinking this mango juice actively but you don't tell anyone else that you love this juice and you enjoyed a lot having it, a strong message of 'I can pay complements' won't be sent to your subconscious mind, since you have not actively given a complement to anyone about this juice.

The need to engage in these activities consciously, enjoy them to the maximum and complement afterwards, carries supreme importance and it can't be substituted by anything else. Hence you need to strictly follow these guidelines. This is the reason why you have to choose activities which you like a lot because it is easy to enjoy something you like and then give complements about it. More you keep consciously enjoying a variety of small but your favorite activities and more you keep complementing, more is the number of messages sent to your subconscious mind that you can enjoy and pay complements. Hence more are the chances that you are going to recover from this negative habit at the earliest.

With time, you may start complaining less and you may start finding reasons to enjoy things and then say good words about them. This is because your subconscious mind has been told again and again that you want to enjoy and pay complements. Accordingly, it starts helping you in enjoying more and complementing more. For example, you go to a party and instead of making complaints about a food item which has not been cooked properly, you may move on to next food item which tastes really good. You may enjoy this food item and you may say good words about this food item. Compared to this, you made many complaints about the bad food item in the same situation you faced some time ago.

Nothing seems to have changed in the situation itself, which means you came across a bad food item at a party just like you did some time ago. However, the way you react to the situation has changed completely and that is what makes the difference. Earlier in the same situation, you chose to make complaints about a bad food item and spoil the fun for yourself as well as for the others, in addition to promoting your habit of complaining too much. Now you have decided to ignore the food item with problems and instead enjoy other food items which are good; and then say good words about them.

You see, the magic has happened and it has not happened due to anything changing from outside but it has happened from inside. Earlier, you had a subconscious script of feeling dissatisfied and making complaints in most situations. Through conscious acts, you sent so many messages of enjoyment and complements to your subconscious mind that it now wants to find reasons to make you enjoy and give complements. It means that earlier, you stuck to anything that seemed to bother you and you started making complaints about it whereas now you choose to ignore things which are not good for you and instead find, engage in and appreciate things which are good for you.

This is why more and more conscious acts of enjoying and appreciating various activities are required to treat this problem effectively. Each time you enjoy and appreciate, you tell your subconscious mind that you want to feel happy and you want to appreciate. Accordingly, your subconscious mind starts finding ways to make you feel happy and say good words. That is why it encourages you to ignore food items or any other things which are not good and it instead motivates you to find something else which is good.

Hence all you've done is changed yourself from inside and the results outside have changed, though the situations remained the same.

Always remember that the outside world will be full of good as well as bad things. In order to get rid of habit of complaining too much, you can't wait for all the bad things or flaws in things and people to disappear because that has never happened and that is never going to happen. The solution to this problem does not lie in finding flawless or perfect things and people, but it lies in ignoring the ones you don't like and instead finding, enjoying and appreciating the ones you like. The world is not going to change much from outside but your world can always change from inside. That is why Heaven and Hell lie within you and not outside.

As you keep enjoying more and more things and people, and as you keep appreciating them, you will start getting rid of complaining too much and you will start developing the habit of complementing. This is the exact opposite of what you had before.

Being Overambitious

Ambition is one of the most needed qualities as without ambition, the drive to find and establish anything better can't survive. It is due to ambition that human race has developed a lot and we have invented/discovered many good things and resources to make our lives better.

It was the ambition of Wright brothers that we should fly; and see we are flying now. It was the ambition of Alexander Graham Bell that we should be able to speak to our dear ones from distances and we are doing so now. It was the ambition of Willis Carrier that we should be able to feel cold even during the hot temperatures and we are enjoying the gift of air conditioning today.

Hence ambition is a must have quality and without it, you may not even contribute much to the society or the world, since the desire/ambition to do something for others is the first thing you need to do so. However like other qualities, ambition too can create problems when it goes beyond a point and it becomes irrational or impractical. A person having excessive ambition is called overambitious.

Being overambitious is not a good quality and it is a negative quality which can make you suffer a lot on various fronts of your life. It may do so by virtue of making you take wrong and hasty decisions, take irrational risks and run after more and more, instead of enjoying what you have already achieved.

Overambitious people, like people suffering from negative attitude, are one of the most difficult to handle and please people, as they keep looking for more and more. They are seldom satisfied with what they have already achieved. They may fix irrational images of perfection for most things and people in their minds. It is almost impossible for anything or anyone to compete with that perfection as that level of perfection is too good to be true or practical. On the other hand, such people are not willing to settle for anything less than their fixed and irrational perception of perfection. Hence it becomes very difficult for them to feel satisfied in most situations.

As a result, they start seeing flaws in most things, people and situations; and they start making complaints about them. Even if they are not able to find visible flaws and make complaints about something, they may complain how such thing should have been better than it is. Though the thing or person has no visible flaws, they are still not satisfied and this is what makes them difficult to handle, because you may never come up to their expectations, no matter how hard you may try.

Such people may do poorly in relationships as it may be almost impossible for anyone to make them happy. Instead, they may trouble the people near them, with more and more complaints regarding how they are not good enough and how they should try to improve themselves. No matter how hard the other person may try to improve, he may almost never improve himself so much as to meet the expectations of one such person. A time may come when the other person starts understanding that their relationship is suffering not because he has flaws which he can't improve on, but because it is impossible to please the other person, no matter how good he may be or he may become.

Hence the other person may decide to move away from such overambitious person as almost no one wants to be in the company of a person who can never be pleased and who will keep making complaints. This keeps happening with more and more people and as a result, more and more people may start moving away from such overambitious person. With time, such person may project an image of being too difficult to handle or be with. This is when he may find it difficult to convince new people to be with him or work with him.

Apart from the sphere of relationships, overambitious people may suffer a lot in many other spheres of their lives. For example, the career graph of an overambitious person may have many lows which come from time to time due to this negative habit. One such person tends to take irrational and blind risks from time to time, in order to achieve the level of success he wants. Since these risks may be too irrational to bring good results in many cases, such person may end up losing what he already has, instead of gaining what he expects. Even if an odd risk pays out and he gains good ground, it may be short lasted as he may again start taking such irrational risks which can pay once in a while, but which may not pay every time.

Another problem that this habit may cause is that people suffering from it may develop a habit of complaining too much, in most situations. Due to this habit, their images may become negative. At the same time, they may find it difficult to enjoy beautiful things and people. Hence this negative habit should be treated in due time.

Let's try to find out how this habit is formed. Two main reasons for being overambitious are; irrational and too much aspiration; and unhealthy levels of greed. Looking at the first reason, though aspiration is a good thing, too much of it can cause a number of problems. Hence even the good qualities should be in balance as too much of them can cause problems.

Let's find out what gives birth to irrational aspiration. People suffering from too much aspiration lack conscience. Conscience is the virtue which tells us what is moral and what is immoral, what is right and what is wrong, what is rational and what is irrational, what is realistic and what is unrealistic, what is practical and what is impractical, in a given situation. Likewise, conscience helps in differentiating between a number of other opposite sets of traits as well as in achieving balance in approach. Hence conscience can be understood as our overall guide which helps us in making right decisions in day to day life.

Looking at an incident from holy Ramayana, Lord Rama says that he has to forsake the kingdom and go to the forests for 14 years as otherwise, his father will lose his word. He assigns more value to his father's word than the kingdom. This is an act of conscience. Lord Rama has the support of the entire kingdom and even his father, king Dashratha wants him to reject his wish and seize the kingdom. However, Lord Rama's level of conscience is too high to fall for such immoral proposals. Hence he denies them all and he does what his conscience tells him to do; and he goes to the forests for 14 years.

Taking another incidence, Lord Rama is in decisive winning position in war with demon king Ravana and he still proposes that he will stop the war if Ravana comes to him; asks forgiveness for his wrong deeds and returns his wife goddess Seeta with respect, whom he has kidnapped in a deceitful manner. This is an act of conscience. An average person in a decisive winning position may want to kill the man who kidnapped his wife and held her captive for many months. However, Lord Rama doesn't want to do that as his conscience levels are extremely high.

Lord Rama says that if the war goes on, not only Ravana will be killed but so many other people will also be killed, who have done no wrong to him or to his wife. He further says that he does not wish to kill so many people for the wrong done by one person. It means he's not looking for revenge and he is willing to forgive Ravana for the sake of people whose life can be saved by doing so, though the wrong done by Ravana doesn't seem worthy of being forgiven.

Taking an example from Mahabharata, all four brothers of Yudhishthara die because of ignoring the warning from a god and drinking water from his lake. Yudhishthara doesn't ignore his warning and he answers all his questions before trying to drink water from his lake. The god is pleased and he offers Yudhishthara to ask him for revival of any one of his brothers. Yudhishthara asks the god to revive either one of Nakul and Sehdev, his youngest brothers.

The god is surprised at his decision and he asks him to reconsider it, as he knows that they are going to face a war with powerful enemies and Yudhishthara has still not asked him to revive any one of his two strongest brothers Arjuna and Bheema. Hence the god asks Yudhishthara why doesn't he want him to revive Arjuna or Bheema who can certainly help him much more in winning the war?

Yudhishthara replies that though Arjuna and Bheema are indeed the most powerful among all five brothers and they are worth more than any other brother when it comes to war, they are his brothers from the same mother whereas Nakul and Sehdev are the sons of his step-mother. Hence if there is a choice that two of the five brothers should live, one from each mother should live. That is why he wants him to revive either one of Nakul and Sehdev so that both his mothers have at least one son alive.

A strong conscience drives Yudhishthara to do such thing, even though it may cost him a very important war and his entire kingdom. The god was pleased with his answer and he revived all his brothers. While making this decision, Yudhishthara was not focused on his profit or loss and he was focused on what was the right thing to do in such situation. Hence his act was selfless and selfless acts can originate from strong conscience alone.

Considering another example from Mahabharata, all five brothers set out on their journey for liberation after they have won all the battles and ruled the kingdom for many years. As they begin this journey, a dog starts following them and he keeps following them anywhere they go, though the journey is a difficult one through hills, forests and many other difficult places. Years pass in the course of the journey and all brothers of Yudhishthara die one by one during this final journey. Only Yudhishthara is continuing his journey, followed by the dog.

One day, a god appears before him and tells him that this is the end of his journey for this life and he has come to take him to heaven. Hearing this, Yudhishthara requests the god to take the dog also to heaven as the dog accompanied him through his entire journey. The god rejects his request and says that heaven can't be granted to a dog and Yudhishthara will have to go there without the dog. Hearing this, Yudhishthara replies humbly that if such is the case, he also doesn't wish to go to heaven.

The god is surprised and he asks Yudhishthara why does he want to leave heaven for a vain creature like dog? Yudhishthara replies that the dog has followed him throughout his journey no matter what came, with such undivided faith in him, as he had for his lord. He further adds that just as a god can't forsake a devotee who has undivided faith in him, he too can't forsake this dog who has followed him throughout this journey with an undivided faith.

Since they have both covered the exact same journey, it is fair that they both should be given the same results. So either the dog goes to heaven with him or he too doesn't want to go there. This is again an act of strong conscience. The dog was also granted heaven, due to such strong act of conscience exhibited by Yudhishthara. Here again, Yudhishthara is not focused on his profit or loss; and he's focused on what is the right thing to do in the situation.

Such levels of conscience may be very difficult to achieve. The good news is that in order to do good things in our lives, we don't need such high levels of conscience in most cases and we can do with less conscience. The above examples are mentioned to have an idea about what a person with very high levels of conscience can achieve. Hence conscience is the virtue which guides us in telling the right from the wrong. Therefore, lack of conscience is one reason for being aspired too much and that too, irrationally.

This is because, a person with good levels of conscience will always know the difference between healthy and unhealthy, rational and irrational levels of aspiration.

Hence he won't be carried away by irrational aspirations. On the other hand, a person having low conscience wishes and tries to achieve each and every good thing he aspires to achieve. He doesn't bother much whether or not he should try to achieve that thing or even keep wishing for that thing. This is where the problem lies as he doesn't have much conscience to tell him which objectives are right or rational, and which objectives are wrong or irrational.

Let's look at the second reason called greed which also works in co-ordination with the first reason. Though greed is overall not a good trait to have, it doesn't cause much damage until it crosses a certain level. Once it crosses that level and it becomes high or very high, it alone is sufficient to get a person into a variety of problems in many spheres of his life. Unhealthy levels of greed are possible only when one such person has weak conscience, since conscience always stands against greed, just like it stands against too much ambition.

Hence a person suffering from being overambitious may lack conscience and he may have unhealthy levels of greed. Due to greed and irrational aspiration, he aspires to achieve a number of luring things and then he tries to achieve them, whether doing so is just or not. As he sets his eyes on best of the things he comes across, and as he keeps wishing for those things, it may become difficult for him to settle for anything less than what he wants. This is because there is not enough conscience to guide him that wishing for the best is one thing, but not accepting anything less than the best is another.

There is no problem in wishing for the best things and trying for them. However, if you get so much fixed on them that you start comparing everything you get, with what you really want to achieve and then you start rejecting or finding faults with everything you get, it certainly is a big problem. Such an approach can make you feel dissatisfied with most things you achieve. Accordingly, you may start making complaints about most things and people who come your way. As you keep wishing for the best and you don't settle for anything less, you start being more and more restless. This is because what you want is not coming to you and what is coming to you is what you don't want.

Hence you're trapped in a vicious circle. You may think that the only way out of this problem is to actually achieve what you want. However, you may not feel satisfied for long, even if you get what you want. This is because you've written a script of wishing for more and more on your subconscious. Hence it may not take long before you set your eyes on another objective, once you've achieved one of your objectives.

This may continue and you may want an objective, only until you've not achieved it. Once you achieve it, it may lose charm and you may set your eyes on something else. This is because you've trained your subconscious mind to live in the future, since all your ambitions/desires always live in future and they don't have a place in the present.

What is actually happening to you is not a desire any longer since it has been materialized. As you have developed a habit of wishing for more and more, you may not be able to focus on what you have or achieved and you may always focus on what is still there to be achieved. The universe is full of things which can't be achieved even in thousands of lifetimes. Hence there is no end to this journey. It means more and more desires/ambitions are only going to make you suffer.

Since your greed and aspirations are high, you may wish to achieve the best things in many spheres of life, regardless of whether such objectives are rational according to your present circumstances or not. This is because too much aspiration and greed may provoke you to set your eyes on the best things. Since you don't have much conscience to guide you, you may set targets which are too high and irrational, compared to your potential.

As you try to achieve such targets, the chances are high that you won't be able to achieve them through fair practices, because there is a wide gap between those targets and your present status, abilities and resources. You may realize that if you try to achieve such targets through fair practices, you may not be able to achieve them throughout your life. At this point, you are left with two options; be realistic and quit trying for such targets or use unfair practices to achieve them.

Since you have weak conscience and the greed factor is high, you may almost always go for the second option. Hence you may start using unfair practices to achieve your targets and this is where the worst this problem has to offer, comes to the scene.

Let's consider that among all other things, you aspire to have a beautiful villa at a good location. Such villa costs way too much to be achieved by saving money from your current salary or business. Hence you may choose to engage in unfair practices or so to say, criminal activities, so that you may raise the amount of money required to purchase your dream villa. As you start engaging in criminal activities, two things can happen.

The first one of them is that you may get caught and punished for a crime before you have made sufficient money and realized some of your dreams. In the second case, you may make good money for some time and you may realize some of your previously set targets before getting caught, punished and being pushed to a point where your status and resources are even lower than what they were at the beginning. In both the cases, you may end up being punished and pushed to a far lower level of resources as well as status.

In addition to suffering the losses already mentioned, when you engage in more and more criminal activities, you practice more and more bad karmas since most criminal activities are bad karmas and some of them are the worst type of karmas. Such bad karmas add negative energy to your aura. Accordingly, you are destined to face a variety of bad things and punishments in future. However, it doesn't end here and it goes further.

Most people who engage in criminal activities, develop many other negative habits which may come to them because such negative habits are parts and parcels of life of crime. For example, smoking, drinking, consuming drugs, gambling and indulging in the company of paid sex workers are the most common types of negative habits or vices which are parts of life of crime. Accordingly, most people indulging in criminal activities are likely to get some or many of these negative habits. This happens because most people around you in criminal circles engage in these activities. Many such negative habits may be passed on to you by these people, as you already know through the first part of this book that the kind of company you keep is important in giving you good or bad habits.

Most of these people have highly negative auras filled with a variety of negative habits. Accordingly, they may be in commanding positions to influence your aura with their highly negative auras and add specific types of negative energies to your aura. As a result, such negative energies may get added to your aura whether you want them or not. It means that their company influences you so much that you also start engaging in various types of vices. As more and more of such negative habits get added to your personality, you may invite more problems.

The readers who have gone through the first part of this book already know what the disadvantages of having a highly negative aura are, and how hard it may be for a person with a highly negative aura to recover from such negativity. Therefore, you have invited so many problems not only for this life, but for many of your coming lives also. This is because such high quantity of negative energy in your aura is capable of bringing various types of problems and sufferings to you in this life as well as in many of your coming lives.

All this may happen because you have a habit of being overambitious. This habit may bring to you, some of the most serious types of problems and troubles there are. It certainly is too big a price to pay for one negative habit. Therefore, if you have this habit, start working towards treating it before it is too late and this habit takes you to a point where it becomes very difficult for you to come back.

Before looking at the treatment for this negative habit, let's first look into some activities done by a person, which develop and then intensify this habit. Many people suffering from this problem may have a habit of looking at and being inspired by the lives of the people who have achieved so many material resources in their lives. When it comes to people who have achieved such resources, these people can be classified into two categories. The first category has the people who have achieved all such things through fair means though it may have taken them long or very long to reach there. The second type of people have also achieved many material resources and they have done it in surprisingly short periods of time, through criminal means in most cases.

Since the path of the first type of people may be long or very long and since you are already suffering from the problem of being overambitious plus you have weak conscience, you may get inspired more and more by the second type of people and not by the first type of people. This is because the targets and the time required to achieve those targets are the only things that matter to you and the means used to achieve those targets may not matter much to you. Hence whenever you watch, hear or read about these two types of resourceful people, the following things may happen at the level of your subconscious mind.

While going through the lives of the first type of people who have achieved things by fair means, you may consciously start thinking that this path is not for you because you may not have such good abilities and opportunities that most of these people have. On top of that, you may not want to wait for twenty years or even more to reach a good level of success. Hence you send signals to your subconscious mind that you don't want to follow the path shown by these people since you are not willing to wait much, in order to achieve what you wish to achieve. As that happens again and again, your subconscious mind understands this script and it starts discouraging you from watching, hearing and reading about this type of people. Accordingly, you may watch, hear and read about them, less and less with time.

On the other hand, whenever you look at the resources achieved by the people of second type, you are fascinated a lot because they have done it in short periods of time. Two things that these people have in common with you are that they all have unhealthy amounts of greed and weak consciences. So whenever you are inspired by this type of people, you send a signal to your subconscious mind that you like this type of people and you want to watch, hear and read more and more about them. With time and repeated efforts, your subconscious mind understands your request and it starts working according to it by bending you more and more towards the lifestyles and achievements of these people.

A few people among this category may be the ones who have lived a long life of crime, gathered so many material resources and still avoided getting caught or being punished. These people are the ones who may interest you the most and they may become your role models. This is because the only thing that may put fear in your mind when you wish to start a life of crime is the fact that sooner or later, you may be caught and punished. Such exceptional people may give you a reason to overcome that fear.

These people may inspire you that you can pursue a life of crime, achieve so much and even then avoid being caught or punished. This is what may trigger an inspiration so strong inside you, that it is capable of breaking all the barriers of fears of being caught and punished. Hence you may decide to follow this path with solid hopes that you will be able to become like one of these exceptional people.

As these changes are taking place, many other things and activities are also happening simultaneously which may intensify this problem within you. When it comes to watching movies, you may go through a variety of movie genres but you may get stuck to the genre of crime and you start watching the movies in this genre, more and more. Even within this genre, your favorite movies may be the ones where the hero pursues a life of crime, he is able to avoid the punishment and live a happy life in the end, even if by suddenly quitting the life of crime after gathering so many material resources.

This is not just a movie for you and it has given you something new to follow your dream path. If the hero can pursue a life of crime and still be a hero, having a happy ending, why can't you do the same? Suddenly, a movie has changed your world and it has made you look like a hero instead of looking like a villain, if you choose to pursue a life of crime. As a result, you may keep watching more and more of such movies and each time you watch one such movie with great conscious interest, you send a signal to your subconscious mind that a criminal is not always a villain and he can be a hero too. He can achieve so much through the life of crime and still have a happy ending. As you send more and more of such signals to your subconscious mind by watching more and more of such movies, your subconscious mind understands that you want to pursue a life of crime. Accordingly, it starts motivating you for pursuing it.

Apart from watching criminal movies, you may read newspapers or watch the news with great interest, about the people who have pursued a life of crime for a long period of time and they have still been able to avoid getting caught or being punished. Such activities may send more signals to your subconscious mind that the life of crime is good.

Apart from these things; you may watch, read and hear more and more about the best things in many spheres and you may wish to achieve those things. You may watch programs which feature best cars, luxurious houses, beautiful islands, top class hotels, best holiday themes, exotic places; charted flights with many facilities, best liquors, best women and many other best things and people who provoke you more and more to reach out and get them.

All these conscious activities keep sending more and more signals to your subconscious mind that you want to achieve all these objectives and you don't care about which path you follow. Hence a point may come when these signals may write a script on your subconscious mind. This is when you may start walking on a new path, a path which promises you all the beautiful things you want, and a path which in reality may bring a great number of problems and troubles to you. This path may ultimately make you reach a point where you are left with nothing else but sufferings.

Depending on their overall personalities, some people suffering from being overambitious may not engage in crimes. Such people may gather much negativity inside them as they may wish for many such things which they may not be able to achieve. This is because they may have high ambitions but they may not wish to jeopardize themselves by indulging in illegal activities. Hence they may be safer but they may not achieve as much as the other type of people may achieve, especially in the short run.

As a result, the number of unfulfilled desires may increase and this may build negativity inside them. Such negativity may make them find faults with most things, situations and people. This is because nothing may compare to their dream image of it. Hence this habit may either make you engage in illegal/immoral activities or it may make you complain a lot. In some cases, it may do both. Therefore, you should start working to get out of this habit.

In order to get rid of it, you need to strengthen your conscience. Doing so will reduce the element of greed and the number of irrational desires. Let's look at some activities which can help you get rid of this problem. At the first level, change what you watch, hear and read since these are big influences which work toward intensifying or reducing your problem of being overambitious. Stop watching, hearing and reading all such things which encourage you to be overambitious. Instead; start watching, hearing and reading such things which encourage you to have more conscience and balance.

For example, instead of spending your time looking at the lives of rich people, resourceful people and other such people who have achieved many material things in their lives, start spending your time towards knowing about people who have delivered real value to the world. Instead of watching the programs featuring luxury vacations, beautiful cars, private islands, private planes and other such things; start watching programs which offer constructive ideas about how you can contribute more to the society and how you can make yourself more balanced/better.

History is full with examples of noble people who have served so much value to this world, who had very high levels of conscience and who set great examples to inspire many people to follow them. Get connected to more and more such stuff so that it may influence your subconscious mind to inspire you in moving towards the right path and not towards the wrong path.

When it comes to movies, avoid watching movies where the hero plays a criminal and he still escapes punishment in the end. Instead watch movies in the genre of crime, where the hero is a noble character and the villain faces maximum punishment for his crimes. Such movies may inspire you to be like the hero and at the same time, they may scare you that if you choose to follow a life of crime, you are going to face severe punishments like the villain in the movie.

These are positive and constructive fears and you should use them to your advantage as they can stop you from engaging in crimes and/or other types of unfair practices like cheating and deceiving. In the beginning, you may find these activities difficult/boring to engage in. With time and efforts, you may start liking them.

Apart from that, start engaging in such activities which are small but at the same time, which are capable of giving you happiness and satisfaction. In order to do so, recollect all the small things which you used to like a lot, or which you still like a lot and start engaging in them more and more.

For example, start listening to or watching your favorite songs, start playing your favorite computer games or video games, start going to gym if you like it, start swimming if you like it, start watching comedy movies or TV programs, start visiting and meeting such friends and relatives whom you like a lot, start going out more to eat some of your favorite foods at places which are not expensive, start eating more potato chips, chocolates, ice creams and other such favorite items, and start doing all other such things which you like and enjoy doing and which don't need much money or resources to be done and enjoyed.

As you keep doing these activities, a sense of responsibility and conscience may start coming to you, through the first set of practices as you watch, hear and read good and moral stuff instead of engaging in luring stuff. The second set of small activities may help you enjoy more often and feel satisfied more often without spending a lot. As more and more such messages of enjoying and feeling satisfied are sent to your subconscious mind through these small but specifically targeted conscious activities, your subconscious mind may start helping you stay away from being overambitious and engage in immoral or criminal thoughts and practices.

This is because the primary reason for you being overambitious is that you want to feel happy and satisfied by achieving all the top class things that you wish for; and you think that happiness is possible only when you achieve those things. In thinking so and in doing so, you subconsciously start keeping yourself away from all such small activities which can give you small amounts of happiness every now and then. All this happiness combined together can actually match or even surpass the amount of your dream happiness which you may get only when you achieve those big things. The habit of being overambitious may keep you further and further away from happiness because it makes you have a perception that you will feel happy only when you achieve big things. Due to this perception, you may stop working towards getting happiness from small but valuable things.

As you start engaging in such small activities more and more, and as you start gaining happiness through these activities, the pressure for being happy and feeling satisfied may be lifted to a great extent. Whatever big you wish to achieve, whatever big you want to experience, the final purpose of all such things and targets is to feel happy. Since you are not able to achieve big things and you are also staying away from small amounts of happiness coming through small activities, you are not getting much happiness in your life.

That is what is making you complain too much, making you feel frustrated and putting more pressure on you to achieve those big things at any cost and by any means. Everyone wants to be happy and more you lack happiness, more desperate you may become, to do anything to get the most needed happiness.

Hence when you keep yourself away from all those small acts of happiness and you are not able to achieve big targets either, for a long period of time, lack of happiness starts building inside you. It makes you more desperate with time and once this desperation reaches a certain level, it makes you complain too much, feel dissatisfied with most things and people; and engage in criminal or immoral activities so that you may get the most needed happiness.

On the other hand, when you start getting small amounts of happiness from many conscious and specifically targeted activities on daily basis, all this happiness keeps adding up and it starts taking care of your need for being happy. Hence the need for taking desperate measures goes down.

Though you may not know why, but as you start getting more and more happiness through these small activities, you may feel that the urge for doing anything good or bad to achieve what you want is getting weaker. This is because the ultimate reason behind achieving all those big things is to be happy. Hence happiness is the final goal whether you know it or not. As you keep getting more and more happiness, you may start meeting your goal. This is when you may get a feeling that you don't need to take desperate measures in order to feel happy.

Each time you feel happy through these small but conscious activities, you send signals of happiness to your subconscious mind. Hence your subconscious mind starts understanding a number of activities through which you can feel happy, as and when you want to do so. With more and more repeated signals of happiness gained through these specific conscious activities, a script is written on your subconscious mind and it then starts working according to that script. This is when you start changing from within.

As a result, the next time you feel the need to be happy and you try to reach out for big achievements but you can't, your subconscious mind may suggest you many small activities through which you can gain small amounts of happiness. For example, whenever you start feeling low thinking about how far away you are from your big goals, your subconscious mind may encourage you to watch a good movie, eat foods you like and many other activities.

As you engage in these activities, they may give you happiness and satisfaction. Accordingly, the pressure on your mind to work desperately in order to achieve your goals is reduced. The beauty of the subconscious mind is that while you feel like going to your favorite eating joints, watching a good movie or doing other things like them, you may consciously not feel that your subconscious mind is doing all this. You may feel like you're in the mood for doing one of these things.

Mood is triggered by the subconscious mind. You are in need of happiness and you have registered many activities which can give you happiness, with your subconscious mind. Accordingly, it inspires you to engage in some of those activities so that you may feel happy. You see, the subconscious can bless you with good moods also. All you have to do in order to get all this is to train your subconscious to help you out, as and when you need such help.

Along with the first two types of activities, you need to simultaneously engage in a variety of third type of activities also as they may reduce the habit of being overambitious from a different angle. In order to engage in these activities, start visiting/meeting such people who have one type of physical disability or another and start spending some time with them even if it is five minutes a day.

When you start doing that, you may realize that there are many people in the world, who don't even have one tenth of good things that you have and many of these people are happy even then. A feeling of gratitude towards God and destiny may come to your mind. You may begin to think that you are blessed to have a healthy body and you are able to enjoy much more than many other people.

Every time you engage in one such activity and every time such thoughts come to your mind, they send signals to your subconscious mind that your life is not all that bad and you are already much better than many people. As these messages of gratitude and being better than many people are conveyed to your subconscious mind again and again, it registers them and starts acting according to the new script.

The next time you tend to have those overambitious thoughts and you start getting restless by thinking that you have not achieved anything till now, your subconscious mind may send inner voices to you. Such voices may say that you are already much better and happier than many people and even your current achievements are much bigger than those of many people. As these voices inspire you, you may start feeling relaxed.

One big reason for being overambitious is that you keep comparing yourself to people much higher and much more successful than you. This makes you sad and desperate because you are the one with least number of achievements, in such comparisons. Hence you wish to compete with them and reach the level of success they have achieved, though such level may be too high and irrational to be achieved by you through fair practices, in a short period of time. As a result, you start feeling like a loser and you start preparing yourself for taking desperate measures so that you are not the one to finish last in this race between you and such very well established people, you are comparing yourself to.

Hence all you need to do is to start running in a different race every now and then. This race is the one where you may finish first and other people running with you may be left behind or far behind. When that happens, you may get a feeling which is the exact opposite of the feeling you get when you compare yourself to people much higher than you. The first type of feeling is a feeling of being a loser and that of being the one who has been blessed the least in a particular group of people. On the other hand, the second type of feeling is the feeling of being a winner and that of being a person who has been blessed the most in a particular group of people.

You see, the solution is simple. If you can't finish first in a specific group of people and you don't think you can either do so in a short/significant period of time, it is the time to change the group and start playing in the group where you can finish first and where you are a big achiever. Your achievements have not changed at all, but merely by changing who you compare yourself with, you have become a winner instead of being a loser. You have become the most blessed one in a group, instead of being the least blessed one in a group. Doing so may not kill your ambitions and it may only keep them in check, by making sure that they are rational and you can afford all the time it takes to fulfill them.

Hence if you are getting inspired by the lives of right type of people, you are getting small amounts of happiness through various activities and you are comparing yourself to the people much below you than the ones who are much higher than you, your habit of being overambitious may start losing strength. This is due to the reason that the combined effect of all these activities may heal you on different levels.

The first type of activities stop you from being inspired by wrong type of people and they help you take your inspiration from right type of people. The second type of activities start supplying you with more happiness and satisfaction so that you don't lack these essentials and you don't feel like taking desperate measures. Finally, the third type of activities tell you that you are not a loser or the least blessed one and you are much more blessed than many people. As a result, you may start having the right type of motivation, you may start getting happiness and you may start being more grateful for being blessed much more than many people.

Accordingly, you may start having more patience to achieve your big targets and you may even start adjusting such targets so that they are relevant and you may achieve them in a decent amount of time. Hence you may redefine your goals so that they are rational and they are worthy of being achieved through fair practices. At the same time, you may develop patience to wait for as long as it takes to achieve them through fair means. The habit of being overambitious is going now and the habit of being rationally and patiently ambitious is replacing it.

Right type and right amount of ambition is a good and a must have quality as it helps you define your goals and it then motivates you to work and achieve them. Since your goals are defined and rational now, they may be achievable through fair means. You are willing to put in the effort required, you are willing to wait patiently through the time required and you are getting due amount of happiness and satisfaction on regular basis. Hence you're focused, relaxed, happy and patient.

Even if you have the ambition to rise sky high, there is nothing wrong with it and it is fine. Ambition in itself is not bad no matter how big it may be. It becomes bad when you are not willing to put in the amount of effort required and more than that, you are not willing to wait patiently in order to achieve your goal. Hence you need to avoid irrational and immoral goals, you need to keep working to achieve your goals and you need to wait patiently to achieve your goals. This is because even if you wish to rise sky high, you will rise only step by step in most cases and you are not going to fly to the skies suddenly. Hence don't be desperate and wait patiently for your dreams to be realized and whenever you reach one step closer to them, enjoy it, celebrate it and feel happy.

Another point worthy of being mentioned here is that desperation and impatience come when you keep sacrificing too much for a goal, for a long period of time and you still don't achieve it. When that happens, you start getting impatient and desperate because you have sacrificed most other things for a goal and even that goal is out of your reach. This is what puts a lot of pressure on you and you start thinking about taking desperate measures.

In order to avoid falling in one such situation, reduce the number of sacrifices you are making for a goal, find and fix ways to get happiness and satisfaction every now and then; and you will start having more patience and being more relaxed. As you are not sacrificing too much for your goals and you are getting your due share of entertainment and happiness, life is no longer work and punishment only; and life now offers enjoyment and happiness also. This fact makes you grateful, relaxed and patient and when that happens, you are in a much better position to achieve your goals.

Coming back to the activities of the third type, apart from meeting people with disabilities, start meeting people who are materially less blessed than you, as that may also create the same effect on your subconscious mind. Meet and interact with poor, deficient and other loss suffering people. You may start being more and more grateful for what you already have instead of cursing yourself or your fate for what you don't have. For example, meeting someone poor or very poor may make you feel grateful for how resourceful you are, comparatively. Similarly, meeting a person with troubled marriage or broken marriage may make you feel grateful for what a good marriage you have.

The world is full of a variety of different people. Whereas there may always be people who are happier or much happier than you in some spheres, there may also be a great number of people who are blessed less or much less in certain specific spheres, compared to you. Hence the correct approach doesn't lie in always looking at better people and feel sad as well as dissatisfied with what you have. It lies in looking at people below you and feel satisfied for how blessed you already are, and then looking at the people above you and try to upgrade yourself to one of the upper levels.

Balance is everything in life and a balanced approach always works the best. Looking only at people much higher than you can make you become overambitious and dissatisfied with your life. On the other hand, looking only at the people below you can make you quit all ambition and effort to rise higher since you may start thinking that you are already blessed a lot and you don't need more. Hence you should look at both types of people. You should have a feeling of gratitude by looking at people less blessed than you whereas you should take inspiration by looking at people blessed more than you.

You should stay away from bad company as indulging in bad company may not only reduce the speed of your recovery, but it may also land you into trouble. This is due to the reason that by virtue of being overambitious, a part of you is already provoking you to engage in unfair practices to fulfill your ambitions. Hence the last thing you want is other people telling you to do the same. Therefore, you should stay away from bad company as such people may encourage you to engage in bad karmas. You have high chances of falling for their bad advice, since your position is already vulnerable by virtue of being overambitious and desperate.

Hence stay away from bad company, engage in all the required activities and you should get out of this habit. Keeping company with positive and wise people may help you a lot and it may speed up the process of recovery.

Being too Greedy

Though greed is not a good trait to have even when it comes in low quantities, it is certainly one of the worst negative traits that you may have when it comes in high quantities.

Greed alone is partly or fully responsible for giving birth to a number of other negative habits. High amounts of greed can make you engage in more and more bad karmas, thereby adding more and more negative energy to your aura.

Though greed initiates through a series of conscious acts practiced by a person, it can soon become a habit. It means that the person suffering from it doesn't have to do any special efforts to be greedy and he starts acting greedy on natural basis. Once a person becomes too greedy on natural basis or so to say, once a person develops a subconscious script of being too greedy, various types of troubles/problems start coming to him. This is because greed can invite many negative habits on its own.

Greed initiates when a person engages in a small act of greed for the first time, though such act may have been practiced more out of need than out of greed. For example, when a person snatches someone else's food or money for the first time as he is in great need of such food or money, he sends a message to his subconscious mind that snatching other people's possessions is fine as it can fulfill your needs.

After some time, this person snatches, steals or wrongfully acquires again, what belongs to someone else. By doing so, he again sends a message to his subconscious mind that getting things you need is important and how you get them is not important. As he keeps engaging in such acts of wrongfully acquiring what belongs to other people, he sends more messages of greed to his subconscious mind. Finally a time comes when a script of being greedy is written on his subconscious mind. This is when this negative habit is born. Hence he starts engaging in such acts naturally/subconsciously. More he engages in them, greedier he becomes.

You may have seen movies where a character tells some other character that once upon a time, he was a poor and needy person or child, he didn't have sufficient resources to make his ends meet and no one was willing to help him out. Hence one day, out of sheer need, he decided to steal or snatch so that he may satisfy his needs. This act fulfilled his needs on temporary basis and after some time, he started having needs again. Since nothing else was working for him and since the act of snatching or stealing had already worked for him, he decided to try it again and so he stole or snatched again.

As the needs kept appearing from time to time and as he kept fulfilling them through snatching or stealing, he ultimately found himself in a habit of snatching or stealing. Hence he kept engaging in these practices even when he didn't need to do so any longer. Now that this character has more money and resources than he needs, he is still snatching/stealing. It all started from need but now greed has taken place of need. Now this character is not engaging in such acts because of need but because he has developed a habit of being too greedy.

The same happens in real life also. In fact, what we see in movies is nothing but a reflection of what happens in real life, in many cases. This person snatches/steals for the first time, because of need and then he does it second time also for the same reason. As he keeps doing this again and again, he keeps sending more and more messages to his subconscious mind that snatching/stealing is fine and there is nothing wrong with it. As more and more such messages reach his subconscious mind, they write a script of being greedy and getting anything through any means. So it all started with need but soon it developed into a habit of greed and this person could not know when his sense of need was replaced by a sense of greed.

As being too greedy has now become a habit, this person keeps looking for acquiring more and more through any available means, though he has gathered much more than he may need in order to meet his day to day needs. As he keeps engaging in acts of greed, he keeps becoming greedier. This is because with each act of greed, he sends a message to his subconscious mind that he wants more, irrespective of how much he already has. As more and more such messages reach his subconscious mind, it encourages him more to snatch/steal what other people have.

This is when this habit may prove troublesome, as it may now be almost impossible for him to satisfy his greed. This is because no matter how much he gathers, he still wants to get more and in fact, more he gets, more he wants. This is due to the reason that each one of his acts of getting more intensifies his problem of being greedy. Accordingly, his subconscious mind starts encouraging him to gain and gather even more. He has now fallen into a vicious circle because his habit of being too greedy wants him to get more and as he gets more, this habit intensifies even more.

This is the reason why you see that some corrupt politicians and some other people having positions of advantage or authority of some kind, keep engaging in acts of corruption in order to gather more and more money and assets. An average person may wonder why these people are doing the worst type of things in order to gain more money when they already have huge amounts of money with them. The money which they can't spend in their entire lives, the money a big part of which is lying in anonymous bank accounts in some foreign countries; and the money, most of which will never be used by them and it will become waste after their deaths.

So why are these people engaging in more and more bad karmas and they are adding negative energy to their auras when they have almost no chance of enjoying the pleasures which can be had through extra money, since they already have much more money than they may need for their entire lives.

As these people keep engaging in acts of corruption in order to gain more and more money, they keep sending more messages of greed and 'I need more' to their subconscious minds. These messages intensify their problem of being too greedy, because their subconscious minds start encouraging them to gain more money by any means. Hence they have become the travelers of a never ending journey. The only thing that can stop them now, is their engagement in a series of conscious acts which can first weaken and then erase the script of greed written on their subconscious minds.

As greed increases, it starts creating/intensifying many other negative habits also. A person with unhealthy amounts of greed is prone to have negative habits like being too selfish, since greed promotes selfishness; being overambitious since greed promotes immoral ambitions; feeling dissatisfied more and more since greed can never be satisfied and on the contrary, more you feed it, stronger it becomes; engaging in acts of corruption, other immoral or illegal acts, engaging in company of bad people since greed intensifies all of these problems too; and many other negative habits.

Have you wondered why richest criminals in the world and all other people engaging in criminal activities engage in more and more bad karmas when they have already achieved more money and resources they may ever need throughout their lives? The answer is greed, greed and more greed. As these people keep engaging in acts of greed, they keep becoming greedier. Accordingly, it becomes increasingly difficult for them to disengage themselves from such criminal activities. Hence they don't stop as they simply can't. By virtue of such karmas, they may get caught and receive punishments.

But even at this stage, most of them may not realize the wrongs done by them. In case some of them do realize that they have done wrong things and they should stop doing them, this feeling may be temporary. They are likely to engage in more acts of greed once their punishments are over, in most such cases. This is due to the reason that though they have realized the wrongs done by them and they wish to disengage from doing bad karmas, the strong script of greed written on their subconscious minds has not been erased. As long as the script of greed is present on their subconscious minds, they may not disengage from bad karmas. Hence they need to find ways to get rid of excessive greed and only then they may be able to move away from crimes.

Looking at another sphere where a person can suffer big losses by being too greedy; relationships are also affected adversely when a person is too greedy. A person who is too greedy, generally doesn't want to give any of his possessions away, even to his close relatives. This is because the script of greed written on his subconscious mind encourages and helps him whenever he wishes to add something more to his collection whereas the same script opposes and resists him when he tries to give away some of his possessions.

Since he has written a script of snatching more and more from people, his subconscious mind feels uncomfortable when he tries to give away some of his possessions. This is because giving away is the opposite of snatching or gathering. Hence the subconscious mind is not comfortable with executing such actions. Therefore, his subconscious mind puts resistance whenever he tries to give away some of his possessions. As a result, he may not be able to give away or share much with most people. As a rule, bigger is the possession in question, stronger is the resistance posed by subconscious mind and accordingly, more difficult it is to succeed.

Hence he may not give away much, though he may have big amounts of money and possessions. Due to this reason, most people may not feel comfortable in his company as they are often not rewarded as much for their good work done for him, as they should be. If he can afford to give away a lot and he still chooses not to do so, this may add insult to injury, as he is well capable of rewarding other people but he still chooses not to. One such person may not be comfortable spending much money even on his wife and children, as he has a habit of collecting more and more for himself and he doesn't have a habit of giving away, which is the opposite habit.

For this reason, even his close relatives like wife and children may not respect him much and they may keep complaining about his habit of saving too much and spending too little. His wife may not be happy in his company and his children may turn rebels because he may not give them their due share and they may feel being deprived of what they duly deserve, most of the time. Such experiences happening repeatedly over a long period of time may spoil the relationships. Ultimately, he may not have many people who love/respect him. This is the price he's paying for being too greedy.

Hence if you have this habit, you should start working to get rid of it. Let's look at some conscious activities which can help you get rid of this habit. The basic principle is to do the opposite of what greed encourages you to do. Since it encourages you to collect, you should start giving away. Hence you should start with small acts of kindness where you give away parts of what you possess.

Start by giving away small amounts of your possessions like money and then build up from there. Stick to the guideline which says that at any level, you should attempt tasks which are somewhat but not a lot more difficult than what you can handle. If you try to give away a lot in the beginning, your subconscious may pose strong resistance and you may fail.

As you engage in repeated conscious acts of kindness and sharing, such acts may send messages to your subconscious that you wish to share/release your possessions. With repeated acts and time, such messages may start replacing the script of greed on your subconscious and they may start writing the script of kindness. Since kindness and greed lie in opposition to each other, their sum total within you is always 100. It means if you're 80% greedy, you're 20% kind. As the percentage of kindness increases, the percentage of greed decreases.

Hence you don't need to focus on not being greedy and you need to concentrate on being kind, as kindness alone will kill greed. It is like if a room is filled with darkness, you don't need to think about how to get such darkness out of the room. You simply need to find ways to bring light to the room. Light and darkness always amount to a total of 100, when added. It means if a room is 100% dark, there is no light. If it is 80% dark, there may be 20% light. Looking at the other extreme, when it is 100% filled with light, there may be no place for darkness. Hence don't try to fight darkness and try to bring light as the latter will take care of darkness on its own.

As you engage in more and more conscious acts of kindness and sharing, the script of kindness may become stronger. When that happens, the script of greed may become weaker. Whenever you become comfortable with a level, increase the resistance gradually. This way, you can start with small acts of kindness and you can build up to significant acts of kindness, with time and conscious efforts. Finally a stage may reach when you may turn kind; and unhealthy amounts of greed may leave you.

This is when you may share a lot with your loved ones as well as with other people. When that happens, the quality of your life may improve a lot. Since you're willing to share money and resources with your wife and children, your relationships with them may improve. It is not about money alone and it is much more than that. When you choose to give priority to money over your loved ones, you send them a message that they don't mean much to you. This is because money is dead and it is not alive.

Hence when you choose to give priority to a dead thing over living people, you convey to them that they have no value for you. By default, everyone wants to be of value to the people he's with. When your wife and children feel that they have no special place in your life, their subconscious minds may reciprocate this behavior of yours. It means you may stop having any special place in their lives also.

On the other hand, when you share a lot with them, you convey to them that they are much more important to you than dead things like money and resources. Their subconscious minds receive this message that you value them a lot. Accordingly, they reciprocate by assigning a lot of value to you. Hence they may start loving you more and respecting you a lot more. Respect always needs to be earned and you can never get it through any other way.

Being too greedy may restrict you also, when you try to spend money and resources in order to enjoy good things in life. That may deteriorate the quality of your life. As you start being kind to other people, you become kind to yourself also. Hence you may start spending money on yourself also. This may improve the quality of your life since you may now be able to enjoy a lot of things that you couldn't enjoy earlier; because of being too greedy.

Apart from sharing money, you can share a number of other possessions you may have. The idea here is to share and give away. Since money is the most valuable possession among non-living things, being able to give it away means you may be able to give away almost everything. This is why sharing or giving away money may prove more helpful.

However, you can share other possessions also, as doing so may help.

With time and repeated efforts, you may become less and less greedy; and you may become kinder and kinder. Finally, you may reach a stage where you don't have to put conscious effort in order to be kind, as you may become naturally (subconsciously) kind. It means the script of greed has been replaced by the script of kindness.

When that happens, you may have to put conscious effort if you wish to be greedy, because the script of kindness may pose resistance. This message has been conveyed many times that whatever you write on your subconscious, it may act according to that. There is no right or wrong for the subconscious and it only believes in executing/expressing what it has.

Hence choose wisely what you write on your subconscious. Through your own conscious efforts, you can make your subconscious your friend or enemy. However in both the cases, the choice is always yours and not that of your subconscious mind. Hence don't blame it if bad things happen to you, because you're the one who created them and you're the only one who can stop and replace them with good things, through your conscious efforts.

Lack of Trust

Lack of trust in most people, things and situations is one negative habit which is increasing with time. As a result, more and more people are falling preys to this habit. Many people think that it has become difficult to trust most people in the present times.

Accordingly, such people choose a safer way to operate, which is not to trust most people they meet or interact with. Some of them may not even trust people close to them. Not trusting people and being doubtful most of the time may save you from being cheated and getting hurt in many situations. However, it may also keep you away from a number of beautiful people, things and situations.

It is like you build walls around you to protect yourself from bad weather, natural disasters like storm, animals and bad people. This set of walls is called house. Though a house can protect you from a number of things and people, protection is always two ways. It restricts outside things and people from reaching you and at the same time, it restricts you from reaching them. As a result, you may not be able to enjoy beautiful weather, scenic views, open sky, fresh air and a number of other things; unless you keep sufficient provisions in such house.

Hence you may choose to have doors, windows, rooftop, lawn, balconies and other such things which help you enjoy a number of things as and when you want. This way, you try to balance security and natural beauty. If you have a house which doesn't offer windows, balconies, lawn or open space and rooftop; you may be derived of some of the most beautiful things which exist in nature. Hence a house stops outside things/people from reaching you but it also stops you from reaching them; unless you've made provisions. The same theory works in case of lack of trust. When this habit becomes strong, you may build many walls around you; with no windows, doors and other such things which may help you connect to the outside world.

Most people suffering from this habit may believe that people are not worthy of being trusted. They can share many such experiences when they trusted people and such people hurt them in a number of ways. Hence they stopped trusting people.

Let's see how this habit is formed. When a person gets hurt/cheated by someone he trusts, for the first time; he may react broadly in two ways. If his overall mindset is positive, he may not care much and he may move on. If his overall mindset is negative, he may think that not all people are worthy of being trusted. The one with positive mindset may not develop this habit and the one with negative mindset may.

As he thinks so, he sends a message to his subconscious mind to be cautious when dealing with people. Over time, he may come across many people as well as situations which may hurt him or he may end up getting hurt. After each one of such experiences, he may send messages to his subconscious that people/situations should not be trusted. With time and repetition, such messages may take form of a script. This script is that of lack of trust. Once it is formed, it may become difficult for him to trust people, things and situations. As this script gets stronger, the problem may aggravate.

As a result, he may not trust most people around him, including the ones who're close to him. Instead, he may doubt most people around him as he is afraid that most people may hurt him if he trusts them. When that happens, he may face issues in profession, relationships and other spheres. This is because in order to make the most in any sphere of life, you have to trust people, you have to give them responsibilities; and you have to believe in them. Without doing so, almost none of your relationships whether professional or personal, may work in the best possible ways.

Since you may not trust people with important jobs or responsibilities and you may not believe what they say or do, people around you may notice it with time. Some of them may try to gain your trust by doing many things for you whereas some others may choose to move away, as they may feel uncomfortable in your company. Almost no one wants to be with someone who doesn't trust him/her, even after years of being with him/her and doing so many things together.

This may be your defense mechanism which protects you from getting hurt by other people. However, this defense mechanism has reached a stage where it is hurting people in order to protect you from getting hurt. It means the problem has not been treated or cured but it has only reversed the donors and recipients. Earlier you trusted people and got hurt whereas now, you're hurting people by not trusting them even when they duly deserve it.

People who have strong habit of lack of trust may naturally (subconsciously) express it through their daily activities. For example, such people are likely to; check a glass or cup filled with some drink and make sure if the glass or cup is not dirty from any place; hesitate a lot in having any drink or some other eatable offered by someone else if this item is new for them and they don't know much about it; and feel uncomfortable or respond negatively if someone requests them for using their cell phones, laptops or other personal gadgets for short periods of time on account of some urgencies.

Likewise, one such person may not pay attention to someone's advice even when such advice is good. He may also not offer help to unknown people in need, like he may not give lift to someone he doesn't know, even if the other person has an emergency.

Looking at more examples; such people are likely to, regularly watch such movies or shows where people get hurt by trusting other people; not share most of their intimate feelings and experiences even with the closest people in their circles; and not accept new friend requests on social networking portals, even if the person is from the same gender and already has a good number of mutual friends.

They are likely to, have a limited number of friends on social networking portals as well as in real life; not share their food with other people and not eat from other people's food like when many people are eating from the same plate; neither wear someone else's clothes/shoes nor offer their own clothes/shoes if someone else wishes/needs to use them; feel uncomfortable when one of their friends meets another one of their friends and they both wish to meet and know each other more often; and do many other such things which exhibit lack of trust in almost everyone and everything, on a subconscious level.

Likewise, there are hundreds of other such examples. As a guideline, more is the number of such day to day activities, stronger is the habit of lack of trust. When this habit is strong or very strong, the affected person may not trust most people and he may crosscheck even the smallest of jobs they may do for him.

As this habit gets even stronger, one such person may start doubting even himself. Hence he may double-check many of his own activities also. For instance, he may lock the door when he leaves house, start to move away and then get back to make sure that the door is locked. Likewise, he may lock his car, move away and press the lock button on the remote after walking some distance, to make sure that the car is locked. He may count money twice whenever he receives it. Similarly, he may engage in a number of other such activities which indicate his lack of trust in people, things, situations and even in himself.

It should be noted that most people have some weak spots or vulnerabilities and that doesn't make them lack trust. Hence if someone engages in a selected few of such activities, he may not lack trust. However, if there's a pattern and he does so in most spheres, he has this habit. For example, someone may have a troublesome shot-term memory. Hence he may double check the door locks and/or car locks. However, he trusts people and situations without any issues. It means he doesn't lack trust but he has issues with memory and he ensures that he's doing important activities twice, in order to be certain.

Likewise, someone may have emotional attachment with his clothes or shoes and he may not share them with anyone. Looking at another probability, he may care a lot for personal hygiene and he may not believe in eating from other people's plates. Similarly, various people may have some of such things which they may do in their own special ways. They may not have habit of lack of trust as long as there are no patterns.

For instance, one such person may not share clothes but he may share money, car, apartment and a number of other things with his friends and relatives. It means he doesn't lack trust. Likewise, one such person may not eat from other people's plates but he may trust them with important jobs and he may believe in them completely. Hence he doesn't have a habit of lack of trust. Therefore, when trying to diagnose this habit; you need to look for patterns and not for isolated events. People who have this habit may exhibit lack of trust in most spheres of their lives; as well as dozens of times a day.

Once this habit becomes strong, people may get uncomfortable in your company. Hence some of them may maintain distance whereas some others may move away from you. Since most of them may not tell you why they're doing so as they may find it offensive saying so on your face, you may not even realize why most people keep distance from you or leave you. This may not help your problem and on the contrary, this may aggravate it. This is because you doubt that people are not worthy of being trusted and this is how you see them behaving.

It means you see them getting closer to you and then you see them move away, for no obvious reasons. This may aggravate your problem and you may become more careful that you don't let people get closer to you, since most of them move away. This is where your problem has become serious. You don't trust people and you let them get closer with difficulty. However, they move away after some time; reasserting your belief that they are not worthy of being trusted. Here again, the cause and effect have formed a vicious circle and one is feeding the other. Lack of trust pushes people away from you and as more people move away from you, you doubt more.

As a result, you may build even stronger walls around you. This is because you may decide that it is better not to let people get closer to you, than letting them get closer and then seeing them move away. With time, you may naturally become very good at keeping people away from you. You may think your defense mechanism of 'don't get closer if you don't want to get hurt' is working properly; the situation may altogether be different in realty. You're not protecting yourself from people, you're pushing them away. It means in trying to avoid getting hurt by them, you're hurting them and at the same time, you're aggravating your habit of lack of trust.

Hence you need to engage in conscious efforts in order to get out of this habit at the earliest as otherwise, you may eventually lose all your loved ones and you may not be able to make new friends or relationships. Let's see what losses you may take if you choose to trust people versus the ones you may take if you choose not to trust people.

If you trust people, it is very likely that some of them may hurt you every now and then. If you choose not to trust people, you may save yourself from getting hurt. However, not only you may end up hurting many people by not trusting them even when they are trustworthy, but you may also strengthen this habit. It means you may keep yourself away from the company of many good people who may bring a number of good things to you, if only you're able to trust them.

Suppose you choose to put your trust in 10 people. Suppose 3 of them betray your trust, 6 of them neither betray you nor do a lot for you; and 1 of them proves good for you and he justifies the trust you put in him. Though the number of people betraying you is three times more than the ones who are faithful, the net results may still be favourable. The ones who betray you are not going to be there with you after they do so. It means you may move away from them. However, the ones who are faithful are going to be with you for long time or for life.

It means that on the path of trust; betrayals are momentary whereas faithfulness is long lasting. Hence you're gaining a lot and you're not losing. Though three people can hurt you three times or even thirty times before you choose to leave them; the one who's faithful may do wonderful things for you, hundreds or even thousands of times throughout your life.

Memorize this important lesson that failures are single events, which means you don't repeat something once you know you are going to suffer through it. On other hand, success is permanent, because you keep doing time and again; what you know works for you. Hence even if 100 failed experiments can lead you to one successful experiment, you're not losing and you're gaining a lot. You won't repeat your failures but you'll repeat your successes again and again.

Hence if you choose to stay away from people due to fear of getting hurt, you may end up paying much more than you may gain. When you go to vegetable market, you see all types of vegetables. You choose the ones you like whereas you leave the ones you don't like. Though there may also be some poor quality vegetables in the market, you don't stop going to the market. You find a suitable solution by choosing the good ones and ignoring the bad ones.

Similarly, you go to an apparel showroom, you select the items you find good and you reject the ones you don't find good. Though there may be some items which are far below your standard, you still keep visiting the showroom, you ignore the substandard items and instead choose the ones according to your standards. Going deeper, suppose for any reason, a showroom owner cheats you by giving you defective items and he then refuses to return such items. In such case, you may at the most stop visiting such showroom and you may not stop buying clothes.

Likewise, you may switch to another mobile service providing company if your current service provider keeps troubling you. Similarly, in many other spheres, you experiment with a variety of things. You move away from the ones you don't like and you select the ones which suit you. You do so because deep down you know that you can't leave an entire practice, if an experiment goes bad. For instance, you can't stop buying clothes if a seller cheats you. Life doesn't work this way and you have to keep moving, no matter what comes.

This is the basic mantra for a happy life and you can't ignore it if you wish to live properly. If you choose to move away from an entire sphere because of some troublesome experiences, you may end up buying no clothes, vegetables, mobile phones, vehicles and most other things. Having none of such things means almost having no life. Hence you keep moving despite setbacks. You experiment in every sphere, you discontinue the failed ones and you keep engaging in the successful ones.

You simply need to do the same in case of people. Keep experimenting and keep interacting with people. Keep the ones who are good for you and leave the ones who cause problems. To move on despite setbacks is the spirit of live.

You don't stop eating tomatoes because a few rotten tomatoes have come to you hiding among good ones; you don't stop wearing shoes because a pair of shoes has torn apart within a week after you bought them; you don't stop using mobile services because a mobile company has robbed money from you; and you don't choose to stay fallen because you have fallen third time in the last ten minutes. Likewise, you simply can't stop trusting people because some of them have breached your trust and hurt you.

So don't worry much about who hurts you or how many people hurt you and keep moving. Learn to experiment, select, reject and then move on. Keep the selected ones and leave the rejected ones, but keep experimenting.

If you are still not motivated enough, do a small but valuable experiment. Mix any type of edible grains with many other items which are not edible and some of which may be garbage like very small pieces of iron, plastic and other such things. Make a mixture in a ratio so that the grains are only 10% of the mixture and the remaining 90% is non-edible items. Throw this mixture over a place where birds may access it. Soon you may find out that though the mixture is full of non-edible items some of which may be potentially harmful for birds if eaten, birds are still coming in great numbers. They are carefully selecting grains from the mixture and they are eating them, whereas they are leaving all the junk items put in the mixture.

This process will keep going and soon you will find that the birds have searched for and eaten all the grains whereas they have rejected everything else which is 90% of the mixture. Some of these birds may try a few other items also, which may be new for them, like very small pieces of plastics which may resemble something edible. However, they may realize soon after trying such items that they are not good for them and they leave such items. Hence the birds come, select and eat ten 10% of useful items whereas they leave 90% of the mixture after finding that it is useless for them.

Now repeat this experiment and reduce the percentage of grains in the mixture, say to 5% this time. The birds will do the same, eat the grains and reject the remaining 95% of mixture. Even if you make a mixture with only 1% grains and 99% non-edible items, the birds are smart enough to select 1% grains and reject 99% non-edible items.

Stick to a mixture of 1% grains with 99% non-edible items. Keep offering such mixture to birds on daily basis. You'll find that more and more birds are coming, they're eating the grains and they're leaving the rest. The best part is that you may find out that the birds are happy and cheerful, instead of being sad or frustrated. Though you're offering them 1% useful items mixed with 99% useless items; they're still thankful to you. This is because they understand that 1% is better than having nothing. A difficult opportunity is much better than having no opportunity at all. Hence they focus on what is suitable for them and they don't bother about what is not.

According to a negative mind, they should curse you for making their job so difficult by mixing 99% useless items with 1% useful items. Hence their chances of success are about 1 in 100. However all you may find out is that they're grateful to you and that is why they're coming again and again, in increasing numbers. You're giving them an opportunity and that is all that matters to them. Whether such opportunity is easy, difficult or very difficult doesn't matter to them.

Compare this situation with the one where you don't offer the birds anything at all. You may realize that though the first situation is difficult to handle for them, it still serves them value and it rewards them for the efforts done by them. However in the second situation, they get nothing at all. Though you save the birds a lot of trouble in the second situation by not making them select a small percentage of mixture with great difficulty, they still don't like this situation as there are no rewards for them. On the other hand, they welcome you every time you offer them a new challenge, because they know for sure that they are going to be rewarded in the end, and that is what matters the most.

You see, even the species like birds have learnt this most valuable lesson of life by heart that difficult or very difficult opportunities are still much better than no opportunity. Success alone counts and failures don't, in the long run. Hence you should learn to welcome the 1% that you like and not bother about the 99% that you don't, in case the scenario is that difficult. Even in one such case, you'll gain in the end and not lose, provided you keep playing.

Hence learn to experiment, do new things, meet new people, trust more people, get rewarded and get hurt also; because this is how life is meant to be. If you have to pick one out of two choices where the first one is die sitting on the shore being scared of going into the ocean and the second one is die drowning in the ocean, always pick the second one. This is because if you choose to die sitting on the shore, you will die achieving nothing or even attempting nothing.

On the other hand, if you choose to go to the ocean, explore it as much as you can and then die drowning, you have given yourself a lot. You have attempted new things, you have achieved new things, you have continuously engaged in karmas and you will die the death of a fighter and that of an achiever instead of dying the death of a scared or fearful person who has done nothing special with his life and he dies a loser.

Looking at a loser, the one who tries his best and fails is not a loser at all, in any sense. Trying hard is a big achievement and even failure is an achievement. A loser is the one who achieves nothing at all. That is possible only in one condition, choosing not to try at all. That way, you don't gain anything at all, not even a failure after fighting well. Hence he's not a loser who fails after trying because he's won effort and failure. He who has not tried at all is a loser because he's gained nothing at all.

It means loser is not the one who fails after trying to succeed but it is the one who lets an entire opportunity pass by him; without giving it a try. The one who has tried, has failed but he has not lost the opportunity in question, as he has availed it. The one who has not tried has lost in the real sense, since he's lost the opportunity itself. Hence in the deepest sense, to fail is not to lose but not to try at all is to lose. The one who fails is not afraid of taking on a challenge whereas the one who chooses not to engage because of fear of losing is afraid. Hence the one who tries is much stronger than the one who doesn't do so because of fear of losing.

Real success doesn't lie in achieving the best possible result in a given situation, it lies in giving it your best, even if you don't achieve much. You may achieve the minimum but you're much better than the ones who didn't try and you're better than the ones who tried but didn't give their best, though they may have achieved more than you. When you learn to give your best, you may fail or succeed based on various factors; but the ability to give your best may never fail you. That is what matters the most.

An interesting fact is that when you try and fail, you may gain more than what you may gain if you succeed, in many cases. You've failed because there are people who are performing better than you in the same sphere. It motivates you and you try harder. Hence you improve. On the other hand, if you're the best in a field, you may not have much to gain from there as no one seems to motivate you to try harder. Hence you're gaining more in the first situation though the outside results may be better in the second situation. For this reason, you should compete with people who're stronger than you as doing so encourages you to improve yourself so that you may perform like them or better than them.

On the other hand, if you keep competing with people weaker than you; you may not grow much and on the contrary, you may start becoming weaker. Taking an example, suppose you can finish a specific race in 2 minutes. If you run with people who finish it before 2 minutes; this may encourage you and you may try hard to improve.

Hence in a matter of days or weeks, you may end up finishing this race in 1 minute and 55 seconds or less. However, if you choose to run with people who can finish this race in 2 minutes and 15 seconds or more; you may lose instead of gaining. This is because you know that even if you finish it in 2 minutes and 10 seconds, you're going to win. Hence you may not feel motivated in this case; and you may rather feel relaxed. As a result, your performance may drop though you may win the race every time.

Therefore, you don't lose as long as you try; and you gain. Hence start meeting new people, assess which ones can be trusted initially and then give them their due chances. You'll find out that though you may get hurt by some people, you may also gain some good people who can prove assets for life and who you could not have gained, had you not engaged in the practice of trusting people. Don't bother about the ones who hurt you and move on, as this is a part of the process. You'll find roses accompanied by thorns, lotuses accompanied by mud and many other things accompanied by unwanted things. Likewise, you'll almost always find good people hidden among a mixture of many other types of people including bad people.

Just like you select roses and reject thorns; select lotuses and reject mud, select good apples and reject bad ones, select edible part of a banana and reject the peel, select television shows you like and reject the ones you don't, select food items which taste good and reject the ones which taste bad and you select jobs you like whereas you reject the ones you don't; learn to select good people and reject bad ones. The only way of doing so effectively is by trying them all.

More you open yourself to people, more you share, more you gain, more you expand, more you learn, more you experience and accordingly; more you grow on various levels. On the other hand, more you shut yourself off and more you stay away from people; more you move away from life, more you contract instead of expanding; and fewer opportunities you get to share, gain, learn and experience. Accordingly, less you grow on various levels. Hence start meeting, testing and trusting people, as you simply can't choose not to grow, because the ultimate goal of the journey of every soul is to grow more and more. Recognize this goal sooner than later and start working towards achieving it.

Let's look at some tips which may help during this process. When you meet new people, assess them initially and see if they're worthy of being given chances. Some people may make you uncomfortable even within 10 minutes of interaction. Avoid them at this stage, as they may be too much to handle for you.

You may also come across some people who may reveal secrets of people in their circles, during the first or second interactions. For example, when you meet one such person for the first time, he may tell you that his friend standing at some distance suffered from a broken marriage as his wife found out about his extramarital affair. This person is not worthy of being trusted, as he's finding joy in misery of his friend. He's revealing his friend's secrets to someone he's meeting for the first or second time. It means he's going to do the same to you. Hence he can't be trusted.

Whenever you interact with someone for the first few times to assess them, ask him about his friends/

relatives and observe what he says. If he speaks ill about many of his friends and he mocks many of them; he may not be worthy of being added to your circle. A good person may always speak well about his friends/relatives and he may cover their flaws, especially when talking to someone he's not friends with. Friends are the ones whom he has chosen himself and with whom he has shared many good as well as bad times. If he can't speak well about many of them; the problem may not be with his friends and it may be with him. Hence leave him and move on.

Another person may behave very well with people who are superior to him or he benefits through them in some way. However, he may behave badly with people who are below him. It means he's selfish and he's worse than even a person who behaves badly with everyone. This is because the second person is honest. Whatever his nature is, he's expressing it without greed/fear of profit/loss. The first person is greedy, fearful and selfish. He praises the ones who can give him something or who can hurt him whereas he treats those people badly, who can't give him much or hurt him much. Hence leave him and move on.

Looking at next category; you may meet a person who may speak a lot about himself. He may tell you a lot about his heroic deeds and so many wonderful things that he has achieved by virtue of his amazing personality. He may be so full of himself that there may be no space for you, if you form a relationship with him. Loving yourself is good but overdoing it is bad. If he speaks well about himself and he speaks well about a number of other people, things and situations also; you should give him a chance. However, if he talks about himself most of the time, leave him and move on.

Looking at next category, you may meet a person who may complain about one thing or another, most of the time. It means he has a negative attitude as well as a negative aura. Stay away from him as he may transfer a lot negative energy to you through visible as well as invisible communication. He may discourage you from engaging in most things; by enlisting the disadvantages. It means he may pull you back instead of helping you move forward. Hence leave him and move on.

Likewise, there may be some other types of people who you should avoid; especially during the early stages of treating your habit of lack of trust. Doing so reduces the chances of getting involved with some of the most difficult to deal with people, which is good for you. Your trust levels are already low and the last thing you want is more and more people hurting you. Hence choose good people only, during the first stage. Let's look at some signs which may help in finding such people.

At any type of happy gathering, if you come across a person who is surrounded by many people or friends most of the time, provided he is not a celebrity, a very rich person or other such person who attracts people by virtue of something material he possess and not by virtue of his qualities, this may be the person you are looking for. This is due to the reason that in most cases, only those people are surrounded by many people, who have proven themselves assets. Due to this reason, their friends are happy to have them in their lives and they don't want to miss any chance of being close to them.

If this person is in a group of 10 people and you don't know who out of these 10 people; is the one you are looking for, here are some helpful tips. You may be able to observe that among this group of people, there is a person who is the center of attention of most other people in the group. It means that most other people look at this person while saying something, he may do more talking than the others and when he speaks, most people in the group listen carefully and react positively to whatever he says. Moving on, if the average distance of one person from another in this group is 2 feet, you may observe that the two people sitting or standing immediately next to him are maintaining a distance of less or much less than two feet.

This happens because our subconscious minds encourage us to get as close as we can get to people who we really like and respect. It means that people sitting or standing next to him like him a lot. If someone is already being liked a lot by other people, he must have some very good qualities as it is not possible otherwise, in most cases. Now observe if the scene changes and this group or a part of this group scatters. Some members of this group may scatter in ones or twos but this person may still be accompanied by at least one or more than one person.

If you further observe that people who are not a part of this group, are coming to greet and meet this person and they greet him with real smiles of happiness on their faces, you don't need more proofs. This person is definitely worth giving a chance as a good number of people may not pay attention or respect to a person at a gathering, if such person doesn't have some very good qualities.

Moving on to the next category, if you find that a person is not only attending with great care to the people who are senior to him or above him in one way or another, but he is also behaving well with the people who are junior to him or below him in one way or another, he certainly deserves a chance. A person who can respect all people and behave well with all of them irrespective of whether they are above him or below him in some manner, is certainly a good person and he is not a selfish person.

This is because if a person can respect those people and behave well with them, who are not likely to do much for him and who on the other hand, may be looking for some benefits through him like his help or approval on certain issues; is definitely a good person. When you know that you are not going to witness material benefits from a person and instead you may have to help him out every now and then, and you can still respect that person and behave well with him, you are certainly not a selfish person and on the contrary, you are a kind and good person.

In today's world, people who are not likely to give you much and who are instead likely to expect you to help them as and when they need it, are seen as liabilities and not as assets. Hence in this day and age where most people are profit oriented, if someone can respect people whom he may not benefit from, he's certainly a kind and good person. One such person may prove a valuable friend for life. This is because if he can respect and help the ones who don't matter much for him; imagine how far he may be willing to go for the ones he really likes and loves.

Considering the next category, if you come across a person who rarely complains about most things, situations and people, and instead he speaks well about them, most of the time; he is the one you should consider giving a chance. For example, if you meet two people at a party and during the course of conversation; the first person tells you how the lighting is not done properly, how a food item is not duly cooked or overcooked, how a drink is not as hot or as cold as it should be, how the party venue is too small or too big for a gathering like this and other such things; you don't want to give this person a chance. This is because he is all about complaining and that's not what you want at this stage.

On the other hand, you find that the second person is not making any complaints about anything and instead he keeps complementing one thing or another about this party. He may say; this snack tastes very good, the DJ is playing very good music, this dessert is so delicious, this venue has enough parking space, the host has really done a great job by organizing and managing a party like this and other such things. This is your man and you should take interest in him. You see, though both these people are attending the same party which has good as well as bad things, the first person is picking up more and more bad things about this party whereas the second person is looking at more and more good things which make this party enjoyable.

It means that the first person has a negative attitude towards life whereas the second person has a positive attitude towards life. It further means that the first person is only going to bother and trouble you by sending more and more negativity towards you through all his complaints. On the other hand, the second person is likely to send positivity to you. He is likely to complement you and encourage you whenever you do or want to do something good. The second person has a subconscious script of speaking well about people and things, as well as encourage and promote good things done by people. This is why he is worthy of a chance.

Similarly, there are many other types of people who possess many good qualities which are visible from their small day to day activities. These are the people you should consider for building relationships. Though you may still get hurt by some of these people who initially looked good, the chances of that happening are not high. On the other hand, the chances of such people proving worthy of your trust are high because they are basically good and positive people. Dealing with such people at the first level or any level of this treatment increases your chances of success. As you already know by now, more is the number of people who serve you value for your trust in them, more easily and faster you are going to get out of this habit. So pay attention to the first phase of initial assessment of people as it is an important phase of this treatment.

Moving on to the second phase, once a person has passed your initial assessment test and you are positive that you want to continue with him, start doing the needful from your end to ensure that you are slowly but surely moving towards building a relationship with him, where such relationship may be of any kind. The most important thing for better results in the second phase is to start slow, and then build little by little from there. You have a habit of lack of trust. Hence you should not trust people with big things in the beginning no matter how good you may find them during your initial assessment of them.

This is because trusting people with big things right away may not only be too much for you to handle later on as you are not used to trust someone so much, but it can also be a little too much for the other person as he may not expect so much from your side in the beginning. Hence if you are in the phase of building a relationship with someone, let's say you are building a friendship; you should start testing and trusting them slowly and not all at once. For example, telling your new friend about some small flaws in your personality may be a good way to start whereas telling him about some disturbing flaws or incidents in your life may be a bad thing to do at this early stage, as your friend may feel uncomfortable and he may decide to move away from you.

Let's look at some things you may share with or ask your new friend to do for you versus the things you should not share with him or not ask him to do for you at this stage. You can tell him how you love to take your girlfriend abroad for vacations every now and then but you should not tell how your relationship almost broke once when she caught you cheating with some other girl. Similarly, you can introduce your girlfriend to him formally some time but you should not ask him to join you two for a dinner at this stage or even worse, ask him to pick your girlfriend from office and drop her home as you are not able to do so at a given point in time.

Likewise you can ask him to give you a ride home if your car breaks down but you should not ask him to lend you his car for a couple of days, at this stage. In the same way, you can share many of your little secrets with him but you should not share your big ones at this stage. You can ask him to do small favors for you but you should not ask for big ones at this stage; you can trust him with small possessions or secrets that you have but you should not trust him with the big ones at this stage. These guidelines are important and you should not ignore them as otherwise you may end up getting hurt by your new friend or you may yourself decide to move away from him, though he has not done anything wrong to you.

Let's look into some of these activities in order to understand this concept in a better way. If you tell your new friend how your girlfriend caught you cheating and your relationship almost broke once, you are creating a number of problems for yourself. Accordingly, you are increasing the chances that this relationship should fail. Since you have told him a big secret or you have trusted him so much, you may start worrying later whether you should have done so or not, and you may get accompanied by a feeling of guilt also. This is because now there is person who doesn't have a well-established relationship with you but who still knows one of your not so good secrets.

Since you don't have a habit of trusting people and the relationship is not well established yet, you may start worrying that he may share your secret with other people or he may take some undue advantage. At the same time, the friend may actually share your secret with someone else as he may not attach much value to your friendship at this stage.

The fact that you have shared this secret with him at an early stage of relationship, may give him an idea that maybe it is not a big secret for you and so he may share it with others. If that happens, this secret travels and it finally comes back to you, the chances are high that you have lost a friend even before making one. This is because you may see it as a breach of trust and you may not be able to trust him any longer. Trust is the key to any relationship. It means once you can't trust someone, you can't actually have a healthy relationship with them.

Moving on to the next example, asking your new friend to join you and your girlfriend for dinner or pick your girlfriend up from work and drop her home, both are bad ideas and should be avoided at an early stage of relationship. In the first case, during the course of conversation, your girlfriend may intentionally or unintentionally tell him some things about you, which you don't want him to know at this stage. Looking at another probability, your girlfriend may not like this friend much and she may later discourage you from building a relationship with him. In the worst case, your friend may start liking your girlfriend more than he likes you and you have created yourself a new problem.

Similarly, in the second case when your friends picks up and drops your girlfriend, the two of them may develop dislike for each other. Looking at another probability, one of them or both of them may get attracted to each other. In all these cases, you're the one's who's going to suffer. In case your girlfriend dislikes him, she may convince you to move away from him. You may get stuck in a difficult situation.

In case one of them or both of them develop attraction for each other; your girlfriend may abstain since she has an established relationship with you. However, he may not do so since he doesn't have an established relationship with you. Hence if he finds out that your girlfriend is attracted to him like he is to her; he may try to seduce her and the outcome may not be good for you. If that happens; it is not as much of his fault as it is yours.

Whether good or bad, most people choose between two options based on their net values in most situations; if they have to make choices. It means they're likely to choose the ones which hold more value. Hence your friend may try to seduce your girlfriend because you don't hold much value for him at this stage, since there is no established relationship between you two till this point. Hence the value of his liking for your girlfriend may be more or much more than the value of your future friendship for him.

It means when you consider this situation practically, his fault is not much as he simply chose a more valuable option. In addition to that, he doesn't have any serious commitments towards you since the friendship is new. Coming to you, it is certainly your fault to present such a temptation to your friend at this early stage of your relationship when you could have easily avoided this incident, had you not moved too fast.

Looking at a comparison, suppose you build a well-established friendship with this person in a year or two. In this case, even if he finds your girlfriend attractive, he may abstain and he may not advance, just like your girlfriend may do. This is because he has something of good value with you and he may not want to lose it. He may understand that attractions come and go but friendship stays. Hence he may choose you over her. Even if your girlfriend alone gets attracted to him and gives him signs, he may ignore them as he may not want to lose you. Hence move slowly and let the trust build with time.

Following these guidelines can help you during both phases of building relationships. Hence start meeting new people, assess them, select the ones you like and start building relationships with them. Start gradually putting your trust in people. This way, trust may find you and lack of trust may leave you; with time and efforts.

Reasons for Rebirth

There are primarily two reasons for rebirth. The first one is the settlement of good and bad karmas whereas the second one is resolutions/desires.

Let's look into good and bad karmas first. Though it is difficult to achieve exact definitions for them, let's try to understand broader definitions for them. If you engage in an action, speech or thought with the intention of benefit of others, it is called good karma. If you engage in an action, speech or thought with the intention of hurting others, it is called bad karma. If you engage in an action, speech or thought with the no intention or desire, it is called a neutral karma. This concept has been explained in details, in the first part of this book.

Let's see how good and bad karmas cause rebirth. When you engage in good/bad karmas with the sense of a doer, their results bind you. To be precise, you tie yourself to them when you engage in them as a doer. A conscious/subconscious sense while engaging in a karma, that you're doing it makes you a doer. If you don't have that sense, you become a medium and not a doer. Hence you're not judged for such karmas, because a medium is not judged.

It is like you kill a person by shooting him. You get the punishment for murder but the gun doesn't get any punishment. This is because you're the doer as you kill this person of your own wish whereas the gun has no wish and it does what you want it to do. Hence you and not the gun will be punished. Likewise, suppose you as a doctor save someone's life with the help of surgical equipment. You and not the equipment receives the praise since you're the doer and not the equipment. Whether you save someone's life or kill someone with the help of a surgical knife, it remains unaffected since it has no wish of its own. Hence you're the doer and the knife is the medium.

It means that deep down, good or bad karmas don't tie you, you tie yourself to them by being a doer while engaging in them. Since the sense of being a doer is created by ego alone, it means ego lies in the root of all good and bad karmas. Once ego is gone, the sense of doer is also gone and along with that sense, the judgment for your karmas is also gone. It is like if a baby urinates on you, you don't judge him. However, if an adult does the same, you may punish him. This is because the baby has not yet developed the sense of doer. Hence you see him as a medium and not as a doer. On the other hand, the adult has developed that sense and he may be doing so despite knowing that it is bad to urinate on someone. Hence he is judged.

Looking at another example, a tree may give you fruits and shade or it may fall on you and hurt you. In both cases, the tree is not judged since it doesn't have the sense of doer. Likewise, rain may bring prosperity in form of crops or it may bring destruction in form of floods. However, it is not judged in both these cases since rain is simply operating according to the arrangement of elements of nature and it has no wish of its own.

Therefore, if you engage in a bad karma, you are tied to its fruits. Since you may not have all the fruits in your present life, you may be born again to have such fruits. For example, you may kill someone for financial gains and you may escape punishment. Such punishment is pending and you may be born again to receive it. Likewise, you may engage in a number of other bad karmas, you may not get punished for all of them in your current life and you may be born again to receive such punishment.

Taking another example, suppose a contract killer murders dozens of people for money and one day, he's shot dead. Being shot dead may not be sufficient punishment for so many murders. Hence he may be born again to receive due punishment. Similarly, there are a number of other bad karmas which can make you take births after births. They'll leave you only when you stop engaging in them. Once you do that, the pending settlements for the already committed bad karmas may take some time to clear. After that, you're free from one condition which brings you back again and again.

Let's look into good karmas. Whenever you engage in good karmas, you have a conscious or subconscious desire for rewards. Since not all the rewards may be given in the present lifetime like the punishments, you may be born again to receive such rewards. In the next life, you engage in more good karmas with desires for rewards. Such karmas may bring you back again in order to reward you. This may continue life after life until in one life you realize that you don't need any rewards. When that happens, you engage in good karmas but you don't wish for rewards. As a result, you're free from one more condition which brings you back again and again.

Looking at conscious desires for rewards, suppose you make a big donation to a charitable organization and you want the rewards. It means you do this good deed after consciously deciding that doing good deeds will bring more fortunes to you. Hence you've made this donation with the intention for results. Accordingly, it is a good karma and not a neutral karma. A part of your decision to make this donation is to be blessed more. Hence a conscious desire for fruits is there.

Looking at subconscious desires, you may engage in good karmas without conscious desires for fruits. However, if you're affected by the results of such karmas, you have subconscious desires for fruits. For example, suppose you make a big donation to a charitable organization and you don't have any conscious desire for being blessed more or gain more material things in return. When people find out about this donation, they praise you and you enjoy such praise. It means deep down, you were expecting this praise. The desire is not obvious and it is subtle in this case. Hence it is a subconscious desire.

Since you're enjoying praise, it means you may be expecting other good rewards also. Such desire brings you back. It means that in this case, you don't make conscious wishes to be rewarded when you engage in this karma. However deep down, you're convinced that you'll be rewarded. The difference is fine. You don't wish for the rewards but you have a strong feeling that they'll be given to you, even if you don't wish for them. This feeling is the subconscious desire for fruits.

It means you're spiritually much more evolved in this case, but the journey is still not complete. This is because the desire for rewards is still there, though it has become much less obvious which means much weaker. In the early stages of this journey, the desire for rewards may be strong or very strong. As you keep moving, the desire gets weaker. During the last stages, the desire may become very weak which means it may become subconscious. When the journey is complete, even subconscious desires may go away. To be precise, when subconscious desires are also gone, the journey may come to an end. It means you don't get rid of desires after the journey is complete and they have to go away first, in order for the journey to be completed.

This is because it is the journey of desires. As long as there are desires, there is journey. Stronger are the desires, longer is the journey. Weaker the desires becomes, shorter becomes the journey. When there are no desires left, there is no journey. Hence the desires don't go away once the journey is complete and the journey is complete once the desires go away.

When that happens, you may make a big donation and you may not be bothered by the results at all. It means you're not affected when people praise you. Since the desire for rewards is gone now, you've made this donation as a medium and not as a doer. The defining difference between a medium and a doer is that the former doesn't have a wish of his own whereas the latter always does. Since you don't have desires for rewards, you're a medium. It means that in the deepest sense, good karmas don't tie you but you tie yourself to them.

Hence when the journey is complete, you engage in Nishkaam karmas. It means you simply do what is required of you according to the situation; and you are not focused on the results. The karmas done without desires for fruits are called Nishkaam karmas. When you don't have desires for fruits, you become a medium and not a doer. It means that the sense of being a doer lies in the root of all this.

As long as you're engaging in karmas as a doer, they can't be Nishkaam since a doer is always tied to the results. The moment you realize that you're merely a medium, you're free from the fruits of karmas; since a medium is never judged.

At this stage, you may save a number of people or someone may get killed by you. However, none of these karmas can bind you now since you neither wish to save people nor kill them, in the deepest sense. Whatever is the will of universal conscience commonly known as God, you're executing it. Hence you're merely a medium and you are not responsible for saving or killing anyone. Accordingly, you're not tied to the results. As long as this sense is there that you're saving or killing someone, you're a doer and not a medium. It means you'll be judged for good as well as bad karmas.

Let's look into the factor of desires/resolutions. Once you're born, you develop many desires and resolutions to achieve so many goals, to enjoy so many things, to be with so many people and to settle scores with some people. These are resolutions made by you and they're stored on your subconscious. Technically, you can't be liberated until your subconscious is empty which means free from each and every type of desire/resolution. Hence as long as such resolutions are there, your journey continues.

Here again, more is the number of resolutions/desires and bigger they are, more time they may demand to be fulfilled and deleted from your subconscious. Hence longer your journey becomes. As you achieve spiritual growth, you realize that desires are in the root of rebirth. As you become aware about them, you stop creating fewer of them. Creation of desires is directly proportional to the amount of spiritual growth you have. More spiritually grown you are, fewer desires you may create. Hence when spiritual growth reaches the highest level; you stop creating new desires/resolutions.

Among the already created ones, you may be able to delete the ones you can and you may have to fulfill the ones which can't be deleted. For example, the desires which involve you and certain things but not people for their fulfillment may get deleted once you achieve awareness and you don't want them any longer. However, the desires which involve other people and settlement of karmic accounts with them, may not get deleted in many cases; and you may need to fulfill them. To be precise, you may need to let other people fulfill them.

Taking an example, suppose you fall in love with someone and you get married to her. Suppose you have a son. You love your wife and son a lot and they also love you a lot. This attachment grows stronger and stronger with time. Parallelly, you work on spiritual growth. At the end of this life, you've achieved much spiritual growth and at the same time, you have unsettled karmic account with your wife and son.

In the next life, you may achieve a lot of spiritual growth during early years and you may not be much interested in getting married. However, your karmic account with them is pending and you may have to get married to the same woman in order to settle it. Since this desire to be together in the next life was mutual and there is much else to settle, you may have to live through this desire instead of being able to leave it. Hence desires related to things can be left with awareness but desires related to people may need to be fulfilled in many cases.

The desire element is a strong reason for rebirth. In some cases, it can make a soul take many births in order to fulfill a single desire as such desire may require many other factors to be present, in order to be fulfilled and these factors may take many lives to come together. It should be noted that each and every desire of every person has to be fulfilled unless a specific person does conscious effort to erase/delete some desires from his list. In such case, such desires are removed from the list, though it may take long time and much conscious effort in order to do so.

Creation and fulfillment of desires as well as the factors essential to fulfill desires have been explained in the first part of this book.

If your desires are related to things and phenomena, they may be relatively easy since they don't have their own wishes. It means if you have the desire and resources, you can buy any car or other thing which is available for money. However, you can't do the same to a person. You need his/her consent in order to be with him/her. Hence the desire and resources alone are not sufficient in this case and freewill of the other person is necessary.

Let's take an example to understand this concept in a better manner. Suppose you like a woman a lot and you wish to marry her. However, this woman doesn't want to be in a relationship with you. In this case, your desire may remain unfulfilled. In case this desire is strong, which means you keep wishing for her for many years or even throughout your life, this desire may be forwarded to the next life.

Hence you two may be born again during the same timeline and elements of nature may bring you together. Here again, you try to initiate a relationship. If she also likes you in this life, she may initiate a relationship with you and your desire is fulfilled. If she doesn't like you, one out of two things may happen. You may either delete this desire which means you may get over her or this desire may be forwarded to next life. This may continue life after life for dozens of lives; until you either fulfill this desire or you delete it. Hence a desire which involves a person can make you take many births.

Once you're free from the fruits of good as well as bad karmas and you're don't have desires; you're liberated. Liberation is a state of mind or state of being and it is not a state of physical body. It means even when you're liberated, you may be born again, in order to do some specific jobs assigned by the universal conscience. However during one such birth, you stay liberated, since liberation once achieved can't be undone.

It means that from early age in one such life, you don't engage in bad karmas and you don't want the fruits of good karmas. Apart from that, you don't develop desires. Since your previous karmic account is clean and you don't open a new one; you are born liberated and you die liberated. Hence the affairs of the physical body may not affect your state of liberation in this life. Since you don't have the doer element, you're free from good and bad karmas. Since you don't have the doer element, you don't have desires/ resolutions.

You can't be liberated as long as you're a doer and you can't cease to be a doer as long as the desire element is there. The doer element and desire element are closely bound to each other and they feed each other. At times, you may not even be able to tell which one is the parent one. For example, you can't have desires without being a doer. This is because someone must be there to create desires.

Likewise, you can't be a doer unless you have desires. This is because as long as there are no desires, you're not a doer.

Hence you have to be a doer in order to have desires and you can't create desires without being a doer. In the deepest sense, ego lies in the root of them. As ego rises, you start feeling that you're separate from the entire existence. It means that ego alone gives a sense of 'I, you, they, me, my, your and their'. As long as ego doesn't develop, this sense is not there. As long as you're not a separate identity, you may not wish for anything because you're everything and everything is you. Since you can't wish for anything which you already have or to be precise, which you already are, you can't be a doer and you can't create desires.

With ego, you become a separate identity and now you see a lot which is not yours. The moment you feel that you're a separate identity with freewill, you become a doer. Hence the journey of creating desires and fulfilling them begins. Then a time may come when you start working for spiritual growth.

Here again, a moment may come when you realize that you're not a separate identity and you're everything as well as everyone who is there in the entire existence. With this realization, all the desires as well as the sense of doer goes away. When you're already everything that can be there, there's nothing left to achieve. It means the doer is gone and so are the desires. Hence you're liberated.

Contact Details

Website

www.AstrologerPanditJi.com

Facebook:

https://www.facebook.com/HimanshuShangari

Email IDs:

himanshu1847-himanshushangari@yahoo.com

himanshu1847-astrologerpanditji@yahoo.com

himanshushangari1847@gmail.com